NLP and
the New Manager

Ian McDermott and Ian Shircore

Orion Business Toolkit

ORION
BUSINESS
BOOKS

Copyright © 1998 by Ian McDermott and Ian Shircore

First published in Great Britain in 1998 by
Orion Business
An imprint of The Orion Publishing Group Ltd
Orion House, 5 Upper St Martin's Lane, London WC2H 9EA

A CIP catalogue record for this book
is available from the British Library

ISBN 0–75282–076–1

Typeset by Deltatype Ltd, Birkenhead, Merseyside
Printed in Great Britain by Clays Ltd, St Ives plc.

Contents

1 New Managers, new skills 1
➡ In search of the difference that makes the difference 1
➡ The building blocks of success 3
➡ A systematic approach to people skills 4
➡ The case of the cool candidate 5
➡ From task to relationship 6
➡ How new is the New Manager? 7
➡ What is different about the New Manager? 7
➡ In a nutshell 8

2 Key elements of NLP for business 10
➡ To capture the essence of excellence 10
➡ Six keys to success 12
➡ To find the answer, look for the question 13
➡ What do you need to do better? 14
➡ In a nutshell 15

3 Managing upwards 17
➡ What you must do if you want to get on 17
➡ Mapping your system 18
➡ The product is you 19
➡ Developing the action plan 20
➡ Reinvent yourself 23
➡ Choosing direction rather than drift 24
➡ In a nutshell 26

4 Managing your career path   29
→ How to know where you're going and what to do to get there   29
→ What do you want?   30
→ How will you know when you've got it?   31
→ Where, when and with whom do you want it?   32
→ What are the present payoffs?   33
→ Keep your goals up to date   34
→ What do you need to do to make them want to do this?   35
→ Invest in building up your USP   36
→ In a nutshell   37

5 Motivating   39
→ How to make things compelling for yourself and others   39
→ Away from and towards   40
→ Why are bad habits so hard to stop?   41
→ How to delegate motivation: an example   43
→ Motivation myths   44
→ How much of what you don't want will it take to make you happy?   47
→ Ask your people what they need   49
→ In a nutshell   51

6 Getting your own way   54
→ How to get what you need, while keeping people on your side   54
→ The secret of influence   56
→ Dealing with anger and hostility   58
→ Flexibility means never being stuck for an idea   60
→ Making X want to do Y: the algebra of success   62
→ In a nutshell   62

7 Giving feedback, taking criticism   65
→ How to make feedback work for you   65
→ Feedback on feedback   66
→ You have to go wrong to go forward   67

➡ The dos and don'ts of feedback 69
➡ Separate behaviour from identity 71
➡ Don't take it personally 73
➡ Learn from your experience 74
➡ In a nutshell 75

8 Resource management 79
➡ How to marshal your own time and talents 79
➡ Energy to burn 81
➡ Get up and do something 82
➡ How do you handle your stress? 84
➡ Little wins mean a lot 85
➡ How to use the outcome frame 87
➡ The nine-year-old strategist 90
➡ In a nutshell 91

9 Remote management 94
➡ How to retain control beyond time and distance 94
➡ Develop people's competence and confidence 96
➡ Making your mark 97
➡ A craving for connectedness 100
➡ Make people want to be part of your team 101
➡ Direction, faith and energy 103
➡ How can I make my people stand out as special? 104
➡ The self-organising team 105
➡ In a nutshell 106

10 Leading, chunking and delegating 108
➡ From managing to leading: how to increase your influence 108
➡ You're a leader, but how do you do it? 109
➡ The overview and the detail 110
➡ The magic of chunking 113
➡ Stepping up the chunk sizes 114
➡ Go to meet small-chunkers at their level of detail 116
➡ The first step in delegation is self-delegation 117
➡ Living with risks and learning from mistakes 119
➡ In a nutshell 121

11 Catalysts for creativity 125
- How to train your brain to create more possibilities 125
- The power of associative thinking 127
- Who made up that dream of yours? 128
- Use people's metaphors to unlock their creativity 130
- Curiouser and curiouser 133
- In a nutshell 135

12 The power of benchmarking 137
- How to do better than you ever thought possible 137
- Making an inspired choice 138
- Look for the point of leverage 139
- How to benchmark yourself 141
- Remember the million-dollar mermaid 143
- Spend time in the company of excellence 145
- In a nutshell 146

13 Expect the unexpected 148
- You can't control the future ... but you can be on your toes and ready for it 148
- The Dictator's Fallacy 149
- Would other people call you flexible? 151
- Don't let fear stop you in your tracks 152
- List your five fears 154
- Is your past running your present? 155
- Don't get stuck fighting the last war 157
- Change has kept you alive 158
- In a nutshell 160

14 Where to next? 163
- If it works for you, use it now 163
- The tip of the iceberg 165
- A final thought 165

Appendix Training, Tapes and Software 167

Index 171

Chapter 1
New Managers, New Skills

'The only books that influence us are those for which we are ready, and which have gone a little farther down our particular path than we have yet got ourselves.'

(E M Forster, 1951)

➡ IN SEARCH OF THE DIFFERENCE THAT MAKES THE DIFFERENCE

What makes one person capable of selling a £60,000 car when another, equally experienced, sales professional simply cannot do it convincingly? How can a manager distil the essentials of success from the first person's method and use them to help the second? It is possible to do it, cloning the success without having to clone the person. But it takes rather more application than the somewhat hit-and-miss process that goes under the name of 'sharing best practice'.

How can one of three equally qualified applicants for a top management position make his chief executive see him in a completely new light, in which he appears the obvious choice for the post? Without deception, but with a sensitive eye to the unstated, unofficial demands of the job, the subjective elements of the selection process can be enlisted to weight the odds strongly in one candidate's favour.

What does a manager have to do to bridge the gap between the head-in-the-clouds visionaries and the fine-detail miniaturists in her office, to allow them to communicate and work as a team? Mediating between quite different mindsets is one of the key skills of practical management. But it needs understanding, backed up by techniques you can learn and use.

All three of these examples have one outstanding point in common. They present management challenges that can only be met by the deployment of sophisticated interpersonal skills. In the past, these have been regarded as unteachable and unlearnable skills, abilities the 'born manager' inherited or the old hand assimilated from long years of experience. Yet business is crying out for large numbers of managers with these skills, to solve today's problems and tomorrow's. A whole generation of New Managers is wanted to create new structures and methods for the Information Age and we can't afford to wait for genetic accidents or lifetimes of experience to furnish us with the skills that are needed now. NLP – Neuro Linguistic Programming – is exciting because it offers a way out of this situation. By showing how a new way of thinking can help us learn and develop a comprehensive range of these essential 'soft skills', it confirms that the skill shortage can be overcome.

Management is becoming 'softer' – less hard-edged and more people-centred – all the time, not least because in the burgeoning service industries the people costs are usually the largest element in the management budget. The highly structured, procedural approach to management as a pseudo-scientific, fact-based discipline is losing ground fast and the rise of the New Manager is helping to dismantle and update some of these over-mechanical views of how people and companies work. We call it de-engineering the corporation and it can't happen fast enough. As our opening case studies and the other experiences related in this book demonstrate, there is room for huge and rapid improvements in the way people and organisations tap the potential that is in and around them. And the ease with which these gains can be made, with the help of a knowledge of NLP, can sometimes be startling.

➡ THE BUILDING BLOCKS OF SUCCESS

In the case of the car company in the first example above, the nub of the problem was an abrupt move upmarket, which left a sales force used to selling £15,000 vehicles unsure about how to adjust to the rarefied heights of a £60,000 sale. Certain sales people took to it like ducks to water, some even finding it easier to sell the new luxurious vehicle than the more familiar bread-and-butter models. But others found the transition perplexing and had little confidence in their ability to make the sale to this new group of well-heeled buyers. For the managers faced with the need to establish a nationwide sales network, it was a matter of urgency to discover what the most successful performers were doing right and to find ways of transferring this magic touch to the others. It was done by observing, in minute detail, precisely what the best people did. Not what they said they did, for they often weren't consciously aware of how they arrived at a sale, but what they *actually* did.

As well as being interviewed, they were videotaped in action and visited by 'mystery shoppers', and gradually a pattern emerged. The top sales people did less. They talked less and listened more. They allowed more time in the diary for each appointment or test drive. They gave off an air of unhurried, unruffled confidence. They didn't seem to be trying. And yet, on close examination, they were each intuitively taking the buyer through a complete set of sensory experiences to get to know the car in a very intimate, multidimensional way.

They would begin with the visual element, walking the customer slowly round the car to let him or her enjoy and comment on the look of it and even lifting the bonnet to show the intricate, gleaming power plant. Then they would turn to the elements of touch, the tactile or kinaesthetic angles, sitting in the car with the potential owner, carefully adjusting the contoured seats to cushion the customer in customised comfort. On the test drive that followed, the sales people would say very little, letting the car speak for itself, except for a brief pointer to the auditory aspects of this experience with the odd comment to draw the customer's attention to the almost eerie silence as the car swept along. They would also ask how the car felt to drive, knowing that it felt great.

By doing all this, they called into play all the three main sense

channels through which we take in information about our world –
sight, touch and hearing – and made sure the encounter with the
car was firmly represented in all three. People have different
unconscious preferences about which of the sense systems they
attach most weight to – some favour the visual, some the auditory,
some the touchy-feely kinaesthetic. But, generally speaking, the
more of these sensory systems are involved, the more vivid and
complete the experience will be. (The sense systems are also known
as representational systems, because they are the channels through
which we represent experience, past and present, to ourselves, for
instance when recalling a memory.) The top sellers were therefore
hitting all the buttons, instinctively maximising the impact of the
product they were selling. Once this process was recognised, and
set alongside the realisation that 'less is more' seemed to be the key
to success with these buyers, it was possible to select some of the
other sales people and train them up to improve their results. By
modelling, or recreating in themselves, the behaviour and
approach that had been identified as leading to success, they were
able to replicate the achievements of the best.

➡ A SYSTEMATIC APPROACH TO PEOPLE SKILLS

Both the search for models of excellence and the conscious
utilisation of the known facts about representational systems and
people's preferences are key elements in NLP's practical approach
to life and business. They made a crucial difference for the car
company we have been discussing and they have numerous
applications in every area of business.

NLP, or Neuro Linguistic Programming, is a way of thinking
about the world, backed up by a set of ideas, insights and
techniques that have been developed over a period of 25 years. It
has proved extremely useful to an increasingly large and international community of managers and consultants and is now widely
accepted as a force which can galvanise the thinking and performance of those who are open to new perspectives. In a business
environment where the people skills of communication, network-
ing, creativity, leadership and self-management are now recog-

nised as vital for individual and corporate success, NLP offers systematic ways to improve your results.

➡ THE CASE OF THE COOL CANDIDATE

In the second example given at the beginning of the chapter, the in-house job applicant was an executive coaching client, keen to win the promotion that would see him working alongside the dynamic, energetic and entrepreneurial head of the company. Like his two rivals, he was superbly equipped for the post. Indeed, when he was asked to imagine himself sitting in the boss's chair and review the candidates from the customer's point of view, he was crestfallen. 'Nothing to choose between them,' he said. 'Any one of the three could do it well.'

The challenge was to find a point of leverage, a difference this candidate could bring to the job that would naturally make him first choice. And that meant looking at the CEO's particular needs. The candidate's first thought was to improve his skills, but they needed no enhancement. More significantly, it was clear that the job would mean a lot of contact with this vigorous, go-getting boss – and our client, though genuinely enthusiastic, did not come across as a natural sparring partner for a man with this sort of personality. As the probing went on we asked: 'How could you make the boss feel comfortable and supported in your company? How could you make it easy, for example, for him to get more done?' The answer that emerged was quick and spontaneous. The client needed to learn to project his own drive and excitement, to take the lid off his zest and enthusiasm and achieve a closer match between his own energy level and that of the boss, so that he could go at the senior man's pace. With one month to go, there was time for several sessions, during which we coached him to let himself be more open and enthusiastic and less reined-in in an interview situation. He was shown how to come across as more solid and engaged, with a fuller voice and more expression, and to allow his previously restrained hand movements to be both more frequent and more emphatic. As the day of the interviews got closer, his own real enthusiasm for the job started to bubble through. It was possible, too, using a variety of NLP techniques, to show him how to tap into his inner resources, including the memories of past successes, so that he could be the forceful, animated person he wanted to be on the big day.

He telephoned after the interview to say he felt he had done well at matching the boss's energy level, and a few days later he heard the job was his. But had what we'd been doing really made any difference? He felt strongly that the rapport between them had clinched the decision. But that was just a feeling. The proof of this came a month later, over lunch, when he plucked up the nerve to ask his boss: 'Why did you choose me?' The CEO smiled. 'Oh, simple – I knew it would be easy to work with you,' he said.

➡ FROM TASK TO RELATIONSHIP

In today's changing world, the focus of the successful manager's concerns has shifted from the task to the relationships associated with it. It is no longer enough to rely on efficient task execution to get you where you want to go. The task, now, is the relationship. Our third example, the manager whose team is made up of a mixture of top-down thinkers and detail specialists, highlights the need for subtle and effective people skills. To get the best performance and productivity from her people, she will need to know how to translate ideas backwards and forwards between big-picture concepts and fully worked plans, building the working relationships within the group until all the people involved can operate successfully together as a unified team.

Businesses are operated by people. And people are much more likely to want to help you succeed if you know how to establish and maintain rapport with them. When you hear talk about the New Manager, it is the emphasis on 'soft skills' – such as being able to build rapport, to lead and influence others, to create a compelling vision of the future and to marshal your own resources – that is the hallmark of the new breed.

➡ HOW NEW IS THE NEW MANAGER?

There have always been New Managers, though their people skills were necessarily grounded in instinct and intuition. But the tenor of the times has changed. In the past, some managers were a joy to work for and others weren't – you just had to hope that you would strike lucky. And Head Office didn't really care much, as long as the job was done. Now it is different. Our experience is that more and more head offices actually do care now, because it is recognised that being able to establish and maintain rapport with those in your charge, and superiors, colleagues and customers, can have a powerful impact on the bottom line. Soft skills are no longer a luxury. In fact, in all sorts of contexts, they may be the difference that makes the difference.

➡ WHAT IS DIFFERENT ABOUT THE NEW MANAGER?

The New Manager recognises that these people skills are the most valuable asset any manager can develop and that the ability to influence others to achieve the goals you've set is the greatest management talent of all. The New Manager knows, too, that this is not a matter of chance or charm and that the way you handle people, including yourself, is something you can learn to improve.

New Managers acknowledge that their own success depends on supporting other people, so that they can do their best. They understand that control is no longer enough and that fear and loathing, while they can certainly deliver results in the short term, tend to be self-defeating in the long run – not least because your key people tend to leave as soon as they see an opportunity.

New Managers know the old truths. They know knowledge is power. They realise that the more they know about their people, the more potentially influential they can be, and that the more influence you have, the less overt power you need. That is why there is a natural association between the concerns of the New Manager and the promise of better performance offered by NLP. Regardless of how little formal power you may feel you have, if you begin to apply the way of thinking outlined in this book, you will undoubtedly be able to increase and extend your influence.

In a Nutshell **New Managers, New Skills**

- **The difference that makes the difference:**
  - You can clone success, without having to clone people.
  - You can mediate between different mindsets.
  - You can learn to develop your people skills.

- **Business needs the New Manager now.**

- **NLP – Neuro Linguistic Programming – makes sense of the 'soft skills':**
  - De-engineering the corporation can't happen fast enough.
  - Techniques for learning from models of excellence, utilising people's sensory preferences and building rapport make soft skills less elusive.

- **NLP offers the New Manager a systematic approach:**
  - It's a way of thinking that will bring you better results in key areas, including:
    - communicating
    - networking
    - creativity
    - leadership
    - self-management.

- **The focus of management has shifted from tasks to relationships:**
  - Efficient task execution is not enough.
  - Soft skills have stopped being a luxury.

- **Rapport means people will want to help you succeed:**
  - Great management is influencing other people to achieve the goals you set.
  - Success depends on supporting others, so they can do their best.

- **The New Manager is a realist:**
  - Knowledge is power – but the more influence you have, the less power you need.

Chapter 2
Key Elements of NLP for Business

'It requires a very unusual mind to undertake the analysis of the obvious.'

(Alfred North Whitehead, 1925)

➡ TO CAPTURE THE ESSENCE OF EXCELLENCE

As the name suggests, Neuro Linguistic Programming is a synthesis that draws on the work of a number of different disciplines. In particular, it is alert to and assimilates developments in the neurosciences and linguistics. By exploring how our brains perform, NLP offers us ways of changing limiting patterns of behaviour and enhancing those patterns that work in our favour. Whether they work for us or against us, we all have certain habitual sequences of behaviour that we run through many times. These are the programmes which can be changed and enriched using NLP.

You could say that NLP is a form of applied psychology, but that would be missing the point. At the heart of NLP is a way of thinking based on seeking out models of excellence. Since the early 1970s, practitioners have been studying examples of the very best practice in a wide range of activities. The field has grown and broadened and it now offers a body of information and technique that can improve almost anyone's professional performance and personal well-being. Some of NLP's early findings – such as the importance of being in synch with another person and the possibility of achieving this through a subtle approximation of his or her body language, energy levels, posture and gestures – have been incorporated into many conventional management training programmes. In the same way, being able to recognise and work with people's preferred communication styles, as revealed by their choice of language – visual or auditory, for example – has become an acknowledged skill. Techniques have been developed that have proved extremely beneficial to many people. If you have a phobia, for instance, it's good to know that you can be rid of it, usually in a single session, by working with an appropriately qualified NLP practitioner.

NLP has also identified and explored many aspects of people's behaviour that are familiar from practical experience, but little understood. Take 'congruence', for example, a useful concept that's well known to psychologists but not yet generally recognised in business.

Congruence is about being able to walk your talk and being perceived by others as being consistent and all of a piece. It's about being free from the contradictions of internal tension. In a sense, it's an unattainable ideal, because whenever we set a goal for ourselves and experience the discontent that comes from not yet having achieved it, we are creating a certain kind of tension, derived from the difference between where we are and where we want to be. There is another kind of incongruence, though, that comes from an internal mismatch between what we say and what we do, between how we think and how we act. There is a certain poetic justice at work here, because people's knack of sniffing out the fake, the phony, the hypocritical and the two-faced means that this is a weakness and a point of vulnerability. People have a highly developed ability to home in on this kind of incongruence. For example, if you were to take what has been developed in the field of NLP and apply it cynically, just to manipulate people, you would have a very short shelf life in any business setting. There is a world of difference between people who take this way of thinking and use it to advance their own and other people's goals and somebody who sets out to exploit NLP as a bunch of slick tricks. The difference shows up starkly in the way you handle people. For us, it was summed up by a course delegate, who said of his manager: 'She's very clever indeed, and I wouldn't trust her an inch.'

There are already many books exclusively about NLP and there would be little to be gained by repeating here what has already been written elsewhere. If you want to explore the field more widely, we recommend you get hold of a copy of *Principles of NLP* by Joseph O'Connor and Ian McDermott (Thorsons, 1996), which provides a brief introduction to the main concepts. Our concern, however, in this book, is to put NLP to work in a business context. Rather than talk at length about the theory of NLP, we have decided to focus on the key issues managers have sought our help with over the last few years and to look at them from an NLP perspective. NLP is a way of thinking that creates new choices. Its approach moves you from being on the receiving end to being an instigator of events. It is a tool for moving you from effect to cause, and its effects can be highly beneficial to the cause of advancing your career.

➡ SIX KEYS TO SUCCESS

By focusing on a selection of issues that are vital to every manager, this book can help you discover new perspectives and give you more choices. If you follow and actively engage with the processes outlined in the next few chapters, we predict that you will notice this happening in six specific ways:

- *An outcome orientation.* You will experience being in the driving seat more of the time and achieve greater clarity about what you want. Whatever the situation, you will increasingly ask yourself: 'Given these circumstances, what is my desired outcome?'
- *Improved rapport.* You will find yourself able to get on with more people – and a greater variety of people. This doesn't mean you'll necessarily agree with them. Indeed, one practical advantage is that you'll be able to engage with people you don't agree with and achieve productive results.
- *Increased sensory acuity.* You will almost certainly start noticing more. You will set less store by the words people use and respond more to the total package of tone and body language that accompanies the words. You'll know more about what's really going on with people.
- *Enhanced flexibility.* This is both mental and physical. You will

become adept at putting yourself in other people's shoes in
order to gather information, to know more about what makes
them tick. Being able to do this will make you infinitely more
effective. You'll find yourself more at ease with a greater variety
of styles. In the course of a single day, you will find that you
can be highly energised at one point, fast-talking and decisive,
and later be just as comfortable listening in an unhurried way to
tease out what a colleague is getting at.

- *An ability to reframe things.* You will be able to change the
conceptual frame that determines how an issue is perceived, by
changing the meaning that the issue has for you or your
colleagues. When the norm is destabilised, it can make people
nervous, but the unexpected always provides an opportunity for
those with the creativity to seize the moment and define it
anew.

- *Increasing congruence.* With less internal conflict, you will be more
in touch with what is right for you. People's potential is often
stymied by a lack of inner alignment – part of you wanting that
deserved promotion, part of you scared of falling flat on your
face. You will become more wholehearted and more single-
minded in pursuit of what you want.

NLP is a practical way of interacting with the world, not an
academic discipline. The major NLP training syllabus, internationally, is specifically known as Practitioner training. If you succeed in
gaining your certificate, you become an NLP Practitioner – and a
practitioner is someone who actively practises what he or she has
learnt. This learning is not just a bag of tricks that can be acquired
in a one-day training session. The UK's Association for NLP will
not even recognise any practitioner training course that takes place
over less than 20 days. With NLP, the learning is in the doing. And
the doing is the difference that makes the difference.

➡ TO FIND THE ANSWER, LOOK FOR THE QUESTION

Every manager is aware of strengths and weaknesses in his or her
personal armoury. We all know there are certain types of task or

particular meetings where stock responses are not enough, where a sudden rush of energy or inventive ideas is needed to kickstart everyone's thinking. Yet often all that is needed to provoke new answers is the right question – and NLP is very strong on helping you get those questions right. By disrupting people's comfortable perspectives and pushing them towards thinking afresh about familiar issues, the questions we recommend you ask your people can be the catalysts to provoke radical and unexpected proposals. They can help you achieve greater clarity about what you want and what you need to do to get it, and give you the keys that will empower you to release a great deal of the neglected and unrecognised creativity that resides in every office.

If there is one substantial difference between the New Manager and the old-school boss, it is the fact that the New Manager's much-vaunted 'people skills' are supposed to provide the means to tap the full range of resources available in each individual and workgroup. Certainly, a genuine resolve to try to avoid wasting these human resources is likely to be there. But many of these soft skills are not much more than good intentions, without an operational framework of techniques and approaches to allow them to be put into action. Throughout this book, you will find many explanations of the broad principles that govern the ways people interact with other people, with their work, with their hopes and dreams, and with the different aspects of their own personalities. But you will also find a great deal of tried and tested practical advice, derived from both NLP concepts and practice and our more than 30 man-years of consultancy experience in industries ranging from hi-tech computing, financial services, telecoms and pharmaceuticals to heavy engineering, chemicals, oil and transport.

➡ WHAT DO YOU NEED TO DO BETTER?

You probably already have clear ideas about what you would like to be able to do better. If you know you need to pay more attention to your relationships with your own managers and directors, to planning your own career trajectory, to motivating yourself as well as other people and to getting your own way, the next four chapters will offer you a lot of usable, pragmatic guidance that you will not find in most management handbooks. At first, some of it may seem strange. Later, when you look back on it, you may be tempted to think of the same advice as just common sense. At that point, it's worth remembering your original reaction. You can't have it both ways, can you? If it seemed a little odd at first, but then looks like common sense, the chances are that you will have already shifted your ground slightly, as a result of starting to think in a less predictable, more NLP-influenced way.

As you move on to the later chapters, you will be examining various aspects of the biggest management challenge of all – how to get the best out of yourself and other people. There are massive and immediate returns to be gained from applying new skills in this area. And because of NLP's inherently positive approach to the world, the gain comes entirely without pain. You will learn how to improve your ability to handle feedback and criticism, to marshal your own internal resources, to lead and manage in enlightened and purposeful ways, to encourage creativity and to clone excellence itself, without having to create an army of clone-like workers. Yet the only price you will have to pay is letting go of some old habits of thought and behaviour that never did you much good anyway.

If there is one observable effect, above all others, that can be recognised in managers who have come into contact with NLP, it is an increase in confidence. The confidence comes with a new clarity about your goals, a renewed curiosity about other people and a clear certainty that all of us have vast untapped resources that can be brought to bear on the business and personal situations that have troubled us. The New Manager whose skill and under-standing of people and work has been refined by taking on board the lessons and way of thinking that is NLP is always going to be more flexible, inventive and influential than colleagues who have not thought these things through. And if that is not a definition of continuing employability in uncertain times, we'd be pushed to say what is.

In a Nutshell   **Key Elements of NLP for Business**

• **Capturing the essence of excellence:**

  – NLP – Neuro Linguistic Programming – offers us ways of

changing limiting patterns of behaviour and enhancing those patterns that work in our favour.

- Congruence – being able to walk your talk, being perceived as consistent, being all of a piece.
- People home in on incongruence.

- **Find out more:**
  - About NLP from *Principles of NLP* (Joseph O'Connor and Ian McDermott (Thorsons 1996)).

- **There are six keys to success:**
  - Outcome orientation
  - Improved rapport
  - Increased sensory acuity
  - Enhanced flexibility
  - Ability to reframe things
  - Increased congruence.

- **With NLP, the learning is in the doing.**

- **To find the answer, look for the question:**
  - Soft skills are just good intentions, without an operational framework.

- **What do you need to do better?**
  - The challenge is to get the best out of yourself and others.
  - Managers gain confidence from NLP – to be more flexible, inventive and influential.

Chapter 3
Managing Upwards

'Many might go to heaven with half the labour they go to hell,
if they would venture their industry the right way.'

(Ben Jonson, 1637)

➡ WHAT YOU MUST DO IF YOU WANT TO GET ON

What makes people successful at work in today's slimmed-down,
delayered, multi-skilled organisations? Why do so many promising
managers end up jammed tight against a glass ceiling, frustrated,
stressed and blocked from fulfilling their potential? How can those
who see the dangers make sure it doesn't happen to them?

No one has all the answers. But some of the main points are
quite clear. In most cases, for example, it is safe to say that people
whose careers run into this sort of problem rarely find themselves
bogged down because of a lack of formal professional skills and
competencies. If the accountant or the salesman or the seismolo-
gist or the systems analyst or the legal executive or the production
manager needs extra training to cope with the demands of a
changing world, that can usually be arranged. As long as the
benefits to the employer are fairly obvious, in terms of higher
productivity or better work, most organisations will make the
necessary investments in these aspects of their human capital.

People who are not happy about the rate at which they are
progressing, despite having adequate professional skills, often
blame themselves. They try to work their way out of the problem,
when they should be thinking their way through it. Taking on
extra work, putting in extra hours and wearing yourself to a frazzle
doing the same as before, only more so, is not going to solve the

problem. If you have been ignored or underrated or sidelined up to now, more of the same is not going to win you the attention, approval and respect that is needed to put your progress back on the rails. You need to stand back, take an informed and objective look at the system you are working in and start planning how you can make it work to your advantage.

➡ MAPPING YOUR SYSTEM

The word 'system' may seem a little odd here. But using it instead of words like 'company', 'department' or 'office' is helpful, simply because it stops you jumping to conclusions about where the boundaries of your problem lie. There are certain key players who you will need to influence, in order to make your situation take a turn for the better. You will need to identify them, see how their responsibilities and personalities interact with each other and draw up in your own mind – or, better still, on paper – some sort of diagram of the real-life system that surrounds and incorporates your job.

> This is always worth doing and will only take a couple of minutes. Start your diagram with a circle to represent yourself. Mark in your immediate manager, his or her boss and any other influential people you have – or should have – contact with, including relevant people in customer or supplier companies and in other departments. Make each symbol bigger or smaller, depending on how much weight each person's view is likely to carry, and join the people up with lines to represent contacts and connections between them. Include anyone whose opinion of you and your performance could be expected to have a bearing on your future, until you have a realistic sketch-map representation of your working world. This is the system you work in.

As you look at this diagram, it will probably be clear where the system offers you useful points of leverage. If you are not likely to get very far in changing the attitudes of your own boss, would it make sense to try to influence the person he or she reports to? If you had a better working relationship with one key customer, would this feed back into your company and improve perceptions of your abilities? Is there a manager in another part of your organisation with whom you collaborate, on projects or in committees, who might prove to be a significant ally?

Managing upwards is all about recognising the system you work in and making a conscious decision to take control of your fate within it. To do that, you need to be clear about who these key players are, because the next step is to devise a clear game plan for engaging and influencing each of them in appropriate ways. Instead of leaving everything to chance and hoping it all turns out for the best, you are setting out to deal with the realities of the situation, to manage the relationships involved and to manage managers' perceptions of you.

➡ THE PRODUCT IS YOU

You can begin from first principles. All these key players you have identified will either (a) form impressions of you and your competence, or (b) remain unaware of your existence. Your task is to make sure they are aware of you and that that awareness is positive and well-founded. Think of yourself as a product. You need to market yourself. Your aim is to ensure that you have real brand recognition and brand awareness among the key decision makers in your system, so that they know who you are and what you are good at, without having to go through the files or ask the human resources people for your CV.

But you also need to know what you want from them. Where do you see your progress taking you? And over what timescale? What do you want and when? The clearer your vision of where you should be going, the more likely you are to find the way opening up in front of you.

To begin the process of relaunching the product that is you, you must know what the market needs. But you don't have to commission a MORI poll or a Mintel consumer study. You know enough about your 'customers' to put yourself in their shoes and come up with some realistic and useful answers to the obvious market research questions:

- What is it that these people need from me?
- What is it that these people need to know I can deliver?
- How do these people see me at present?

It is well worth taking this minute of inspired introspection seriously, and possibly coming back to it over the course of a day or two. Try to view the questions as *subjectively* as possible from each customer's viewpoint. Differentiate between individuals, so that you do not lump all the customers together in your mind. Deal with each one individually and make notes of the insights you glean, before moving on to the next person's perspective. If you can do it without arousing too much suspicion, why not actually go to your customer's building or to the office and ask yourself the questions while literally seeing the world from his or her perspective? When we talk about putting yourself in someone else's shoes, this is not just an idle figure of speech. The closer you can get to being in that person's place, the more glimmers of insight you will bring back to inform your self-marketing campaign.

Marketing specialists can elaborate to their hearts' content on these questions, and especially the last one. What have you got going for you? What is working against you, in other people's perceptions? If you are viewed as a brand, what would SWOT (strengths, weaknesses, opportunities, threats) analysis highlight about you? What is your unique selling proposition (your USP)? Advanced marketing experts may even like to ask themselves the sobering question: 'Where am I in my own product life-cycle?'

The purpose of asking these questions, of course, is to learn what the market needs and how closely the product matches up to the need. On the basis of this new information, it is now possible to start work on an action plan to improve your situation. Oh, and if you think you're near the end of a product life-cycle, it may be time to invent a new product.

➡ DEVELOPING THE ACTION PLAN

There is nothing mysterious about how your action plan will work. It merely gives you a format for managing key people's perceptions of you, rather than letting them drift or be manipulated by others. But the focus of the plan has to be something substantial, something more than just spin-doctoring or window-dressing. And the central idea is simply that you create opportunities to demonstrate how you can add value, in specific ways, for each of the key people in the system.

Adding value, of course, is a well-worn, even over-familiar business term these days. But that doesn't mean that it has exhausted its usefulness. In particular, it is still valuable because of the way it reminds us that there may sometimes be reasons to assess worthwhile benefits in non-cash terms. Adding profit is a crudely limiting goal. Adding value, as a concept, goes a lot farther.

NLP can give you greater leverage in adding value by 'finding the difference that makes the difference'. Assuming the difference you are going to make is a difference in a positive direction, the notion of adding value is implied here as well. But what this phrase also encapsulates is a reminder of the principle of leverage, the fact that very small forces, acting at critical points in time and space, can create huge changes. Your action plan is aimed at adding value and finding out where you can make a difference.

In a minute, you are going to have to take over and do some of the work yourself. After all, nobody can hope to get a ready-made action plan out of this or any other book. What we can do, though, is help to steer you towards methods and principles that will work for you and increase your control over your business life. In forming your action plan, you have four main goals, two of which are obvious and two rather less so.

The two obvious targets are as follows:

1) Raise your profile with the people who matter in your system
2) Increase the amount of contact you have with the targeted people

If you are not progressing as you feel you should, the need to raise your profile is more or less self-evident, though it is only when you have completed the proper system analysis that you can be sure your efforts are being directed where they will do the most good. Increasing contact is both an end in itself and a way of raising the profile. Simply talking to those you need to influence is important.

Writing memos, exchanging e-mails and sharing information, both official data and unofficial grapevine intelligence, all have significant contributions to make to this strategy.

Above all, though, the big opportunity arises when you spot the chance to ask for advice. No one's door is ever closed to the junior colleague who comes asking for the advice that only specialist knowledge and experience can offer. Busy managers who will not give you the time of day at a meeting are often quite prepared to set aside time and give you their undivided attention while they patiently explain the nuances of their art. What's more, they will frequently offer to lend you books or background papers, spontaneously contact you later on to see how you benefited from their wisdom and even begin to see previously overlooked talents in you, simply because you came to them for advice.

The two less obvious targets are as follows:

3) Make the targeted people's lives easier

Raising the profile and increasing the contacts are both vital. But the third consideration in shaping your action plan is the need to add value, in terms of making the individual's working life easier. This involves looking for ways of helping his or her budgets stretch further, reducing the number of meetings or site visits he or she is required to attend, taking responsibility for unwelcome administrative or training obligations, and so on. Every organisation is different and you will have to look around for opportunities to be conspicuously helpful within the system you work in. What is really important here, though – and not generally recognised at all – is the element of surprise.

4) Create unexpected benefits

However large or small the benefits you are able to bestow on these people, it is the *unexpectedness* of your contribution that will catch the eye. Unanticipated benefits count double; treble, even. So much in business is dull, boring, routine, cyclical. So much is logical, predictable and planned. Surprise them. Make them think:

'Oh, I hadn't really seen this person in that light before.' Show them facets of your capabilities they didn't know you had. Better still, show them facets you didn't know you had. Find ways to demonstrate that they have more of a resource in you than they had ever realised. Force them to reframe the situation and see it from a radically different perspective and you will force them to make a reassessment of you.

➡ REINVENT YOURSELF

The next question is this: if the people you need to influence are going to re-evaluate the product that is you, should the product itself be improved, upgraded or revitalised? You are likely to be moving into more stimulating, more challenging roles. Do you want to be the same person who was champing at the bit and pawing the ground when your talents were being ignored? Arguably not, or, at least, not in every respect.

You don't have to be a chameleon, though conspicuously self-reinventing entrepreneurs like Madonna or Richard Branson or Tony O'Reilly (of Irish rugby, Heinz foods and the *Independent* newspaper) seem to thrive on that. You do have to be prepared to change, and to recognise the fact that in the course of a long career you are going to need to draw on many different facets of your personality. Putting it bluntly, if you stay exactly the same for 40 years, you are hardly likely to maximise your career opportunities and be singled out for promotions. If you want more from life, you have to put more in. That is going to mean using and developing different skills and talents and mastering new competencies at different times. It means making some kind of commitment to your own personal and professional development, quite apart from the purely technical skills of your chosen discipline. You need to consider how you will retrain and even reinvent yourself, possibly several times in the course of your career.

The higher you go in business, the more these technical skills are taken as read. Hard skills and sheer professional competence do not assure you of recognition and rewards. It is all the rest that turns out to be the difference that makes the difference. If you work in computing, you gain no Brownie points for knowing about the Internet. In a mechanical engineering firm or a chain of shoeshops, or a police force, or the upper reaches of the church, your easy familiarity with the Web is far more significant. It underlines your adaptability and the fact that you have not let your mind atrophy over the past few years. It indicates curiosity, patience and an openness to new ideas. It's hard to imagine the circumstances, but it might be a skill that is needed on occasion to solve a particular problem. Whatever else it does, though, it singles you out as an individual from the mass of your peers. Even totally non-vocational skills, such as hang-gliding, sculpting and juggling, help to differentiate you and your experience of life, making people more curious about you and discouraging them from seeing you purely as an instrument for the fulfilment of work-related tasks.

➡ CHOOSING DIRECTION, RATHER THAN DRIFT

If professional skills are taken for granted, what really makes the difference is the whole range of soft skills – communication, influencing, self-management and the ability to motivate others. Strip off the formal labels and we are talking, here, about how you come across as a person, which is the sum of many innate talents, embedded personality traits and consciously learnable skills. For many people in mid-career, with less outgoing personalities and a history of working in 'non-soft', rule-based areas of expertise, this is not necessarily good news.

Example

Gerry, a very experienced financial services compliance officer working in the City of London, has daunting intelligence and expertise. Nevertheless, at the time he sought our help, his career seemed to have reached a plateau. When Gerry spoke, it was in measured, careful, abstracted terms and the general impression he created was reserved, over-controlled and dissociated from the situation in the room, almost as if he were an outside observer, watching the conversation from a distance. This air of dissociation meant that he was not in a position to make his keenness for new challenges show through as a strongly felt enthusiasm. He was unable to project the strong, favourable impression needed to inspire others to trust him with a job at the highest level.

Gerry needed to learn ways of being more engaged in the moment and more present in the room. He needed to learn to talk less guardedly, with less meticulous detail and more understanding of what other people needed to hear. Yet, because many of these changes involved both body and mind — and because changing the one can directly help to change the other, at all sorts of different levels — it was relatively easy to show him how to begin to make a change for the better. Gerry had to start by changing his posture from the cramped, stiff, stillness that had been his style. When sitting, he needed to sit up and lean forward, instead of slouching back and distancing himself from the others in the room. Better still, he needed to be encouraged to move about, to pace around the room as he talked, so that his voice came from a moving body, subject to gravity and Newton's Laws of Motion and aware of its surroundings and the need to avoid bumping into the furniture. By moving to reunite the body and the brain, to stop Gerry from peering out of an inert body and viewing the world as if he were not part of it, his unnerving dissociation could be overcome.

In the same way, he could consciously learn how to talk more engagingly and adapt his mode of speech to his audience. Many of those he had to deal with in the City context were permanently rushed, pressured people, living on a knife-edge. To give them what they needed, Gerry had to learn to summarise, to talk almost in headlines and to put across clear messages very succinctly, sifting information on the basis of his understanding about each individual's urgent concerns. He learnt to feed his colleagues a bulletin of these headline summaries and pick up, from their reactions to each item of news, which ones they wanted amplified and expanded. At the same time, he learnt not to feel flustered by their bustle and impatience and by the abrupt way they would mutter 'Gilmo' ('Got it, let's move on') as soon as they had grasped the gist of his story.

For Gerry, the fact that a few helpful suggestions and a little coaching could give him a lot more control over the impressions he created at work came as a surprise. He had assumed that this was

how he was and that he could not and should not change, as
changing would be disowning his real self. Realising that this part
of what he had taken to be his 'real self' was no more than a set of
habits and behaviours that could be modified to allow other
aspects of himself to shine through was something of a revelation.

Like many people, Gerry had a rather romantic attachment to the
idea that he had been formed a certain way and that any change
that was not 'spontaneous' was wrong and manipulative. Since all
communication skills, from speech onwards, are learned behaviours, this is a perverse and unnecessarily fastidious view – and one
that had led many people to pay a heavy price in terms of social
and family frictions and career frustrations. It is not manipulative
to choose direction, rather than drift. There is nothing pure and
improving about being at the mercy of other people's whims and
prejudices, when you could be taking the initiative in running
your own life. One of the liberating aspects of knowing a bit about
NLP is that it can place in your hands a range of tools that can be
used to widen your options and manage your career, so that you
can take the paths you choose for yourself.

In a Nutshell   **Managing Upwards**

- **What you must do if you want to get on:**
  - More of the same won't necessarily move you forward.

- **Mapping your system:**
  - Draw a realistic sketch-map of your working world.
  - Should you try to influence the person your manager reports
    to?
  - Recognise the system you work in and decide to take control
    of your fate in it.
  - Draw up a game plan for engaging and influencing the key
    players.

- **The product is you:**
  - Build brand awareness, so they know what you're good at,

without having to ask for your CV.

- What do you want and when?
- Ask the key questions:
  • What is it that these people need from me?
  • What is it that these people need to know I can deliver?
  • How do these people see me at present?
- Answer as *subjectively* as possible from each customer's individual viewpoint.
- Go to the office and ask the questions while seeing the world from his or her perspective.

• **What would SWOT analysis highlight about you?**

• **What is your USP?**

• **Where are you in your own product life-cycle?**

• **Develop an action plan:**
  - Create chances to show how you can add value, for each of the key people.

• **Find out where you can make a difference:**
  - Raise your profile with the people who matter in your system.
  - Increase the amount of contact you have with the targeted people.
  - Make the targeted people's lives easier.
  - Create unexpected benefit – unanticipated benefits count treble.

• **Ask for advice.**

• **Find ways to show they have more of a resource in you than they had realised:**
  - Make them reframe the situation.

• **Reinvent yourself:**

– Should the product be improved, upgraded or revitalised?

– Make a commitment to your own personal and professional development.

- **Choose direction, rather than drift:**

  – Soft skills emphasis is no bonus for mid-career people used to 'non-soft', rule-based fields.

  – Learn to summarise, sifting information to meet each individual's concerns.

  – Change for the better does not mean disowning your real self.

  – Widen your options and manage your career.

Chapter 4
Managing Your Career Path

'When the journey from means to end is not too long, the means themselves are enjoyed if the end is ardently desired.'

(Bertrand Russell, 1949)

➡ HOW TO KNOW WHERE YOU'RE GOING AND WHAT TO DO TO GET THERE

It was the late Laurence Peter, author of *The Peter Principle*, who best summed up the realities of career planning. 'If you don't know where you are going, you will probably end up somewhere else,' he said. But there are an awful lot of somewhere elses lying in wait for the unwary, for those who do not decide on either a direction or a destination and who do not make up their minds to go for it.

These days, very few people find themselves working inside the kind of organisation that still offers an internal escalator, a career structure that means you only have to stand still and keep your fingers clear of the handrail to be borne onwards and upwards towards the higher levels. Those who joined such organisations five, ten or 15 years ago have found, more recently, that the escalators have ground to a halt and the nature of the business has become unflinchingly meritocratic. Walking up a stopped escalator is disorientating and harder work than it looks. Standing there and hoping it will start up again is even worse; it means setting yourself up to be a victim – of apathy, of stress, or of the next round of redundancies.

Any career is about movement and progress. If you don't progress, you will eventually feel yourself slipping back. But it is important to be absolutely clear who is responsible for this progress. Your career is your own business. It is your own enterprise, just as much as if you set up a small firm and began working for yourself. Like any commercial enterprise, it needs work, investment, planning, marketing and objectives. And if the objectives aren't sorted out with some clarity, you can be sure all the work, investment, planning and marketing are not going to achieve any significant results.

➡ WHAT DO YOU WANT?

Defining your career objectives is a natural, straightforward process – and one that is surprisingly rarely carried out. It begins with the most obvious of questions and rapidly moves on to raise issues that are fundamental to the way you choose to live your life. Yet the starting point is a simple four-word enquiry: 'What do I want?'

'What do I want?' is always a useful question to ask. But its usefulness is greatly enhanced when you apply a little extra discipline to the way you put together your answer and you add on a couple of important supplementary questions.

The discipline that is required is an insistence that your answer should be phrased in a positive form – not 'I want to get out of this dreadful office', but 'I want to work in an office where people are cheerful and talk to each other'; not 'I don't want to be taken for granted', but 'I want to hear whether my ideas are being taken up'; not 'I don't want people to ignore me when I have a problem', but 'I want people to show me how to solve problems I haven't come across before'. Almost anything that you are tempted to say in a negative way can be rephrased in positive terms. And it is well worth making the effort to do this, because there is a fundamental psychological difference between imagining something positive and trying to pay attention to a negative concept.

To understand why, try this experiment now: don't imagine a blue tree.

Notice how you have to imagine a blue tree, even as you follow the instruction not to. Every time you focus on what you don't want, you recreate it in your mind. But supposing, when you ask yourself what you want, all that comes to mind is a negative formulation, such as 'to stop working so hard'. Though it is formulated in the negative, that doesn't mean it's a bad plan. If this happens, just continue: 'OK, so that's what I *don't* want. And if I wasn't working so hard, what would that do for me?'

The answer might be: 'I'd be able to spend more time with my family.'

'So what do I want?'

'I want to spend more time with my family.'

Now you have an answer you can work with, that is stated in the positive.

➡ HOW WILL YOU KNOW WHEN YOU'VE GOT IT?

If you have answered 'What do I want?' with a reply consisting of positive goals, positively stated, you are now ready for the first subsidiary question, which is: 'How will I know when I've got it?' This is also a loaded, provocative question, with more to it than meets the eye. It gently leads you on to define a highly subjective choice of indicators that will mark your success. For some people, the significant symbols of success are external – public awards, the trappings of wealth or acceptance into a certain social or professional group. For others, they couldn't be more different. These people may crave approval from a parent, the admiration of their children or even an inner sense of achievement that has no apparent outside manifestations at all. Asking 'how will I know when I've got it?' can trigger an exploration of the criteria that motivate a person and the symbols that represent those criteria. Whether for yourself or with others, follow this up by asking: 'What will I see, hear and feel that will let me know I've arrived at this particular destination?' In other words, what specific sensory signals will confirm unmistakably that you've got what you set out to achieve? Sometimes people can be very precise about these things, because they have been rehearsed in dreams. At other times, we need to clarify what our evidence for success will be – evidence that we can see, hear and feel.

Either way, these images can be valuable fuel to carry you

onwards, towards your distant goals. If your dream is to smell the leather as you sink into the chair behind that huge desk on the top floor, or to face the flashguns as you emerge from the law courts after a famous victory, or to hear your CD played on the radio, or to see your book on the shelf in W. H. Smith, this vision of the endgame gives you a real advantage. It puts you ahead of all those thousands of people who feel down, underutilised and demoralised but have no vision of where up might be. Their spontaneous answers to the original question 'What do I want?' will always come out too vague, too relative and too abstract to be useful to them – 'I want to be more successful', 'I want to be better paid', 'I want to be promoted', 'I want to work somewhere else'. The very fact of having a clear, specific idea of what you do want helps to stop you thinking like a victim of circumstance. It gives your ambitions shape and dignity and sets your subconscious processes to work on the problem of making the link between your present situation and the goals you have set your heart on.

The idea that the goals or desired outcomes you focus on should be clear and specific ('What do I want?'), stated in the positive and verifiable through direct evidence from the senses ('How will I know when I've got it? What will I see, hear and feel?') is an important part of NLP's refinement of the widely practised art of goal-setting. By stipulating that goals must be clear, positive and open to sensory proof, NLP pushes people towards the creation of 'well-formed outcomes', which stand a higher chance of coming to fruition than less rigorously defined objectives.

➡ WHERE, WHEN AND WITH WHOM DO YOU WANT IT?

There are other 'well-formedness' conditions that you can add to the list, to help you refine your goals even further. One is to ask yourself: 'In what context do I want this?' In other words, when, where and with whom? What is the ideal time scale? Do you want it all the time, or only in a working context? (You can probably imagine some personal goals – 'I want to be more assertive and competitive', for example – that might be appropriate for work but highly disruptive in a social and family context.)

➡ WHAT ARE THE PRESENT PAYOFFS?

Another important, and often revealing, question is: 'What are the payoffs to me from the present situation?' There will always be payoffs, though they may well be unacknowledged. If you start pushing to change your world without recognising what you might be losing, you may find your subconscious intervening to spike your guns at every turn. You may aspire to advance, but contrive not to do so.

This is what happens to many smokers when they decide, in all good faith, to give up cigarettes. There are so many positive by-products that it becomes really hard to make the change. Companies, too, sometimes find it hard to kick certain habits, for similar reasons. And people's jobs throw up examples of this kind of mixed motivation over and over again.

Example

One junior employee felt it would be difficult to make progress in her present company without sacrificing the friendship of her colleagues. She had formed strong ties with them and believed it would be better to look for a more senior position in another firm, rather than move up, uncomfortably, to a position where she would have to take responsibility for disciplining, or perhaps even firing, her old friends. But she was also loath to leave. The result was that she never quite did what was needed to earn her promotion, but then felt resentful at being overlooked. Only when she started asking herself 'What do I get out of the present situation?' did she realise how she was keeping herself stuck. At that point, she was able to choose to do something different – and for her, that meant going to a new company.

It is vital to identify the positive by-products of the current situation, so that you can devise ways to keep them or take them with you when you go – or, at least, be clear about the price you are paying. And that leads on to another set of subsidiary questions that can be quite crucial for people's happiness: Is the change you are contemplating worth the price you will have to pay? Is it worth the time and effort? Is it in keeping with the real you? Is it something that would seriously affect your peace of mind, your health or your family? It is all too easy to take the wrong career decision when you are mesmerised by the idea of more money, glamour, travel, responsibility or status. But if you fail to take these personal factors into account, you may find your career takes on a life and logic of its own. What you want to avoid is the chilling experience of looking around in a couple of years' time and realising that your career is in good shape, but you are not.

➡ KEEP YOUR GOALS UP TO DATE

It is never too late to begin imagining and defining well-formed career outcomes for yourself. But, whenever you do it, it should not be a finite, one-off process. You need to check regularly to see whether your goals still have a magnetic and inspirational attraction for you. If not, perhaps you have changed, or maybe the world has changed around you. Either way, a goal that no longer excites and stimulates will not be an asset to you and needs to be rethought. Too many people's lives have stalled as they lived on yesterday's dreams.

Once you have developed and refined goals that will work to motivate you, it is necessary to look at the practical implications. Your response to a compelling goal will always be to want to move towards it – that's what makes it compelling. But the next question that arises is whether the outcome you desire is one you can do anything about. Goals are most empowering where you can see some clear possibility of taking action to start and maintain progress towards them. Goals that depend entirely on other people, or the gods, for their fulfilment are not so helpful. If what has emerged from your attempts to define your goal is something that seems to involve helpless – or, worse still, hopeless – waiting, with no possibility of initiating action yourself, you need to explore the situation in detail until you find the point where *you* can take positive steps forward.

➡ WHAT DO *YOU* NEED TO DO TO MAKE THEM WANT TO DO THIS?

It is not uncommon to meet people whose goal could be summed up as something like 'I just want to be promoted'. This, of course, really means 'I just want other people to promote me' and looks, on the face of it, extremely unpromising. If the person is truly committed to inertia and insists on sitting there, changing nothing and hoping others will offer a promotion in recognition of the sheer length of time served, it hardly constitutes a goal at all. Why should anyone want to promote a person who appears so passive? They would be mad to do so. Happily, though, it is very easy to turn this way of thinking around and reclaim the initiative. The point where this person can begin to initiate action towards making good things happen is the point where he or she starts to think 'What is it that I need to do to make sure they will *want* to promote me?'

Suddenly, the scenario is one that admits the possibility of change. And the change could come via many different routes. It could come through the acquisition of new capabilities ('I know, I'll study for the marketing diploma', or 'I'll make sure I'm the one who knows most about EU rules and the new digital technology'), through a new willingness to rise to a challenge ('I'll volunteer, instead of ducking, when the next awkward project is being handed out'), or through the adoption of a more outgoing and communicative approach ('Maybe I should talk to the finance and purchasing people more and find out what their needs are'). Any one, or any combination, of these changes could bring the possibility of the longed-for promotion appreciably nearer. Whenever you find yourself wishing others would do something that would benefit you, instead of just waiting and hoping, turn your thinking around 180° and ask yourself: 'What do I need to do to make them want to do this?'

Thinking like this brings a whole range of other benefits, too. It makes you feel better about your work. It makes other people feel more positive about working with you. The actions that follow will probably make you more visible to your superiors and the rest of the organisation, which is a significant career management goal in itself. This way of thinking will even make you feel better about the non-work aspects of your life, simply because it puts you back in the driving seat and re-emphasises that you are in charge of most of what happens to you. As soon as you decide to invest in yourself and make a bigger impact on the world, the payoffs start to flow in – even before anything much has had a chance to happen.

➡ INVEST IN BUILDING UP YOUR USP

When we said, earlier, that your career was your own business, we mentioned the need for investment and marketing to make your enterprise prosper. And it is the investment you make in yourself that provides the substance to underpin your marketing efforts. On one level, it is obvious that training to use new software packages, taking accountancy exams, learning German at evening classes or making the effort to take advantage of any other opportunities for professional and vocational training is bound to enhance the product that is you. If you have more of the relevant skills, you have more to offer employers.

But that is not the whole story. It is not even the interesting bit of the story. What is far less obvious and far more interesting is the fact that the investment you make in parts of yourself and your life which do not have directly vocational connections also brings returns. People who achieve their career goals tend to be big people, with a big presence. Other people respond to them, notice them, want to please them, want them on their side. The presence and the impression of bigness and conviction and complexity that carry them forward come from a sense of purpose and a strong sense of self. And all this stems from the investment such people make in growing themselves.

Being strong and interesting and fulfilled and successful does not come from hiding from experience, or from knowing and doing only what everyone else knows and does. If you have been stuck in the same place and the same job for several years, is having the same range of experiences year after year going to grow you, as a person? Is it going to make you more promotable? If you are going to run your career, like you would run your own company, you need to be in the business of growing yourself. You need to create the opportunities for new experience, as well as taking the opportunities to learn new skills. Think about what you would really like to do, in work or out of it, and ask yourself why you have not done it yet. Ask yourself: 'If I died tomorrow, what five things would I regret not having done?' If you did do them, what would that do for you? What would you learn or acquire from doing these five – potentially thoroughly hedonistic – things that would actually turn out to be useful personal resources for your career?

There could be unexpected payoffs from taking up needlepoint, restoring a vintage car, visiting Argentina or learning to windsurf or play the tenor horn. Any new experience like this will bring you into contact with different people and encourage your brain to think in different ways, stimulating new connections at both the social and neural levels. Anything that fires up your enthusiasm will contribute towards making you a bigger person. Anything that makes you a bigger person is helping, however indirectly, towards the creation of someone with a real USP, the unique selling proposition we talked about before, a Unique Slant on Problems that makes you all the more valuable to your present employer or in any future job. The line does not always run straight from your investment in yourself to the payoff further up your career path. It may go all round the houses, but the connection is real enough.

In a Nutshell   **Managing Your Career Path**

- **What do you want?**

  – Answers must be phrased in a positive form.

- **How will you know when you've got it?**

  – What will you see, hear and feel that will let you know you've
    arrived at this particular destination?

  – Not only in the positive, but also verifiable through direct
    evidence from the senses.

- **Where, when and with whom do you want it?**

- **What are the present payoffs?**

- **Is the change you are contemplating worth the price you will have to pay?**

- Is it worth the time and effort?
- Is it in keeping with the real you?
- Is it something that would seriously affect your peace of mind, your health or your family?

- **Keep your goals up to date.**

- **What do you need to do to make them want to do this?**

- **Invest in building up your USP:**
  - If you died tomorrow, what five things would you regret not having done?

Chapter 5
Motivating

'Almost every person, if you will believe himself, holds a quite different theory of life from the one on which he is patently acting.'

(Robert Louis Stevenson, 1881)

➡ HOW TO MAKE THINGS COMPELLING FOR YOURSELF AND OTHERS

Motivation is a slippery subject. Motivating others can be hard. For many, motivating themselves is even harder. For the New Manager, knowing how to energise and sustain people's enthusiasm is one of the true secrets of success.

To understand the how-tos of motivation, it is best to examine the inner workings of a real person. And since you are here and interested in the subject, who better than you?

Let's start by finding some examples of things you have achieved, in any area of your life, when you felt highly motivated. These examples could be anything from buying a new house to getting a new job, from organising a special holiday to running a conference. You may have raised funds for a charity or finished a project to a tight deadline, learnt to swim or passed a professional exam. Take a minute or two to think of two examples – one from the working part of your life, the other from outside work. If you can't put your finger on one of each, pick two from work or two from the family and leisure context. If you do this, however, notice what that imbalance seems to imply. Are you only ever strongly motivated at work – or only outside work? What would that say about the nature of your enthusiasms and the rewards you seek? Notice, too, if you think you're more motivated in one of these two areas.

All too often, people don't realise that if you're motivated to do anything, then you do know about motivation. And that's still true, even if what you're motivated to do doesn't seem very useful – motivation is still motivation. You may just need to change what you're motivated to do.

➡ AWAY FROM AND TOWARDS

Once you have identified your case-study examples, choose the most vivid memory and try to pin down for yourself what it was that was especially motivating. Were you moving away from the unwanted, or were you moving towards what you wanted – or both?

It is motivation that prompts you to move an issue to the top of your immediate priority list that makes you decide to get on and do something about it. By contrast, telling smokers in their twenties that they should quit because of the consequences in later life is often a doomed mission, because the time frame involved is too long for them to recognise the linkage between cause and effect. Though they may accept that it is important, the priority attached to it is just too low to motivate them into action. They see no *towards* motivation and the *away from* impulse is too faint, too distant, to seem real.

Yet there are huge, geopolitically significant examples of situations where clear priorities and a powerful combination of the two motivational directions changed the course of modern history. The wave of immigrants who sailed *away from* famine, oppression and poverty in Europe *towards* the land of opportunity in the United States helped create the most ambitious, self-motivating society the world has ever seen, producing a nation and culture that arguably has a strong *towards* bias, even now.

For many people what fires up the warmest urgency of anticipation is a clear, bright vision of what success will be like or an almost tangible feeling of how it will be to achieve the goal. When we look forward to something like this, we draw on our past experiences to bring into play sensory memories of how good we once felt in a similar situation. We project into the future by recreating the past. We feel dazzled or we tingle with pleasure as we imagine, and remember, how good it will be. The feelings are strong and specific and create an almost irresistible promise that hijacks our attention and focuses it on achieving.

The first and most powerful technique for self-motivation uses this process to break through the fuzzy abstractions that normally make future events so hard to concentrate on. You must work, quite deliberately, to summon up this kind of vivid, specific imaginative experience. You do it by drawing on parallels with similar things in the past and reliving – sense by sense, as far as you can, and in as much detail as possible – the memories of how good it felt and what you could see, hear, smell and taste. The art of motivating yourself is the art of building up the full emotional reality of this 'future memory', so that it becomes a completely real, pleasurable and satisfying experience that just happens not to have occurred yet.

When you think back to your chosen examples of past success, it is worth noticing that pleasure is always the key part of the experience. You may struggle through adversity to succeed, but this often only intensifies the pleasure of succeeding. Pleasure is how we measure achievement internally, our internal yardstick of success. We are drawn towards the pleasure, whether it's feeling the kick of swimming that first length or hearing the applause at the end of the conference, just as we try to avoid pain. But the pain/pleasure model of motivation is far less symmetrical than we tend to think.

➡ WHY ARE BAD HABITS SO HARD TO STOP?

Before we go on, it would be useful to set a different kind of example against the highly motivated achievements we've just been discussing.

> Think of something you know perfectly well you should do. Let it be something that would be positive, sensible or even wise to do – and that you know full well you will not do, or not yet, at

any rate. If you smoke, giving up could be a good example. If you bite your nails or blame your parents for everything that happens in your life, dropping these bad habits would do, too. Now, if you know it would be good to make these improvements and you don't do it, why is that? How does the feeling of contemplating this issue compare with the feeling when you remember your highly motivated success story? What are the essential differences?

One is that you will almost certainly have thought about these sensible reforms in purely abstract and wholly negative terms. As we discussed earlier, any attempt you might make to motivate yourself into not smoking, not biting your nails or not blaming your parents for everything is doomed by the practical impossibility of imagining these negative concepts – all you're doing is restimulating the memory of what you actually do. The second key difference is that what you are being invited to do is go away from your present habits. It may be thought of as being *for* your own good (which could, perhaps, be seen as a positive goal, though a dismally vague and ill-defined one), but it is still, in reality, an '*away from*' motion. This is the kind of motivation that is generally associated with the 'pain' half of the pain/pleasure model, where people are seen as fleeing from pain and pursuing pleasure. 'Away from', pain-fleeing motivation can be very strong, right up to the point where you feel yourself to be beyond the range of imminent danger and out of any immediate discomfort, when its effectiveness goes into a sharp decline.

Comparing and contrasting the examples drawn from your own experience, you can draw your own conclusions about what works for you. In the cases where you were triumphantly successful, the strong positive motivation did not, as people sometimes assume, just happen. You made it happen. You motivated yourself as you looked forward to your success, endowing yourself with the unstoppable conviction and confidence that made it almost inevitable. And you can do much the same again, to prime yourself for other positive goals that you really want to achieve.

When people talk about motivation with sticks and carrots, they are using a particular metaphor for one variant of the pain/pleasure model. On the stock exchanges, they talk of the two gods of the market as being fear and greed. Fear certainly sums up the stick end of the equation, though greed is, perhaps, a little harsh as a description of what we might prefer to call 'the promise of better things in life'. The point about the financier's view of the world is that fear and greed are seen as being opposites, in terms of the behaviour they induce. It is assumed that people in the grip of fear sell when those driven by greed buy, and vice versa. In the same way, managers often think of sticks and and carrots as alternatives, as mutually exclusive options. But you don't have to elect to motivate people by either trying to get them to move away from something (with a stick) or towards something (with a carrot). You do not have to choose between one motivational direction and the other, because they can be combined and made to work together. A suitable mixture of the two is the most powerful motivational cocktail, for yourself and for others.

➡ HOW TO DELEGATE MOTIVATION: AN EXAMPLE

If you are ambitious to succeed at work, you know you will need good health and a robust constitution. Physical stamina, the power to sustain concentration and the ability to stay awake and energised for long periods are strengths that matter far more in the upper levels of management than is usually recognised. But are you prepared to make the investment in your health that such a demanding career is likely to require? It's certainly a high risk strategy to assume that you can soak up all the pressure and just take it for granted that the strength and fitness you need will be there when you want them.

Example

One successful New Manager and trainer we know has followed this chain of reasoning to its logical conclusion and motivated himself to do something about it. Partly led by *towards* motives ('I like the way it makes me feel good, look good and have more energy') and partly goaded by *away froms* ('What if I don't? I'm tired of feeling stressed out and exhausted at the weekends now, so what will it be like in another ten years?'), he has committed time and money to an arrangement by which a personal fitness trainer visits him twice a week.

Having thought through all the arguments, he knew what he should do. He was also motivated to do it, but, crucially, not enough to make himself adhere to a strict and sometimes uncomfortable regime that would mean cranking up his own motivation all over again for every exercise session. Just being aware of the upside and the downside wasn't enough – there were always pressing demands on his time, which meant work would always take precedence in the moment. He needed to take a decision and then award that decision a sufficiently high priority for it to affect his routine.

Prioritisation is a vital element in the practical art of self-motivation. Our would-be-fit New Manager was shrewd enough to recognise this. By hiring someone, he effectively delegated the job of maintaining this priority to the visiting fitness trainer, for whom turning up at the right time and being well paid for his expertise is obviously a mainstream career priority.

Prioritisation and motivation are almost inseparable. After all, actions speak louder than words and whatever you find yourself paying attention to is what you have prioritised.

➡ MOTIVATION MYTHS

There are four debilitating and distracting motivation myths that crop up frequently in life and business. People who become involved in staff appraisal programmes will be only too familiar with them, yet they are often allowed to go more or less unchallenged. These myths are described below, together with suggestions for overcoming them.

Myth 1: I am not a very motivated person

No lust, desire for security, need for recognition, craving for love or wanting to eat or drink, then? Hasn't at least one of these at some time caused you to engage in action? Or do you just mean that you're not very motivated within the work context? People often confuse motivation with ambition. You can be very motivated – to get drunk, for example – but that doesn't make you ambitious.

Suggestion

Recognise that motivation is desire manifesting in action. Know that the more confused and conflicted you are, the more you will experience confused and conflicted desires – and the more confused and conflicted your behaviour may seem to others. At the extreme, these wants and desires may be contradicting each other – you want to work through the night to get recognition and meet the deadline, but you also need to sleep because you feel shattered.

Remedy

Get your priorities clear by getting a well-formed outcome and resolving any conflicting impulses.

Result

You will not only have a clearer idea about what matters to you, but also have a stronger sense of who you are. Others will pick this up and feel more confidence in you. You become more of a person in your own right – someone who knows what you're about.

Myth 2: I don't have a lot of motivation

Not quite the same as the above. In its purest form, this is a finite resource theory – 'I can't let myself get motivated about one thing, or I won't have any left for anything else.'

Suggestion

Recognise that motivation is self-generated. It is not a commodity out there, but a natural by-product of desire and requires two elements to be internally generated in your brain – the desire to achieve, coupled with a belief in your ability to make something happen. If you have a desire, but feel helpless or impotent, then you're going to feel undermotivated: 'I'd like to . . . but what's the point?'

Remedy

Start noticing where in your life you *do* have some control.

Deliberately start making things happen within your sphere of influence. Then begin building out from these oases. If possible, get input (coaching or training) on how to have more influence and so become in charge of your world.

Result

You will find the amount of motivation you have goes through the roof. The fact that you now know you can impact your world will motivate you to choose how you will live – because now you believe it is possible.

Myth 3: Motivation is all you need

Romantic nonsense. You are going to need 'how-to' knowledge, too, and the right tools for the job.

Suggestion

Recognise that motivation requires skill in action; you could be very motivated and still not know how to achieve your goal. In these circumstances, trying hard will just be very trying.

Remedy

Get clear about the skills you need to achieve your goal. Maybe you need to speed up the rate at which you process information coming in to you. Would a speed-reading course help? Or can you have someone in the role of gatekeeper, to screen and edit incoming data before it reaches you? Ask yourself what resources you need and how you're going to get them.

Result

You will become far more effective when you know what you need. The more you are able to have an effect in your own world – it could be just signing on for a course to acquire a new skill – the more motivated you will become.

Myth 4: You don't need motivation – just talk money

This ignores so much of what really drives people. People who assume money will be sufficient to motivate often attract people who demonstrate the truth of this assumption – in their case.

Suggestion

Recognise that motivation is not just triggered by external induce-ments. Indeed, the most powerful motivation, arguably, comes from inside, from our own wishes, desires and values – 'I stuck with it because I needed to prove to myself that I could do it.'

Remedy

The remedy is to get curious about what's driving your people. The more triggers, in the form of wishes, desires and values, you know about, the more you can make your requirements relevant to what drives them.

Result

You will become more influential because you will be touching more bases with far more people, much more of the time. The more influential you know you can be, the more empowered you will feel. And the more empowered you feel, the more motivated you will be.

➡ HOW MUCH OF WHAT YOU DON'T WANT WILL IT TAKE TO MAKE YOU HAPPY?

One of the most useful insights offered by NLP is that human behaviour is fundamentally purposeful. People do not act at random. Nor do they act against their own interests, as they understand them. People do things in order to try to achieve what matters to them. It follows that if you want to motivate people, in a work context, you need to understand what they are trying to achieve. This applies just as much in negotiations with outside contractors or customers as it does in the business of trying to manage your own staff. Indeed, it is the basis of all constructive negotiation.

If you know, with some precision, what the other person is aiming for, you have the opportunity to use your imagination and business creativity to search for a solution that is acceptable to both of you. But it is vital to avoid jumping to conclusions. Before you assume a knowledge of the other person's motivation, ask them to tell you what their aims are. You may get the whole truth, some part of it or, in surprisingly few cases, a brush-off or a tissue of lies. Often, though, you will pick up enough new information to move you a step closer to a possible solution or to an effective way of motivating an individual within your organisation.

Once you start talking to people about what they want, it becomes clear that the answer is hardly ever just a matter of money. It often happens that individuals, and collective bodies such as trade unions, enter business negotiations stridently demanding more money, when it is actually a surrogate for other things that are wanted far more urgently, such as better working conditions or pension arrangements, shorter hours, longer holidays or more involvement and autonomy in the workplace. In such circumstances, if the employer conducts the usual ritual dance of wage negotiations and eventually concedes a straight pay increase, no one's real needs are met and the stage is set for the same charade to be acted out again next time.

You cannot satisfy people just by giving them money. We all want it and we tend to think we want more of it, but it is no coincidence that a large body of accumulated research evidence shows that pay levels are far from being the most important drivers in motivating people to work – well behind less tangible elements such as job satisfaction, companionship and job security. We feel good if we can become involved and become part of our work, and if our work becomes part of us.

This is why the idea of 'ownership' of a problem has become such an important factor in management thinking in the past decade. To motivate people so that they will be willing to bring all their effort, talents and energy to bear on a problem, all you often need to do is make it clear that it is theirs. If you are in a situation where someone will volunteer to take it on, all well and good. If not, you will need to hand it over to someone who may not be quite so pleased to receive it. But whether it's a hopeless case, a ticking bomb or a chance for a young manager to forge a reputation, you need to make clear that it is being handed over for good or ill. There is nothing more demotivating for the person who takes up the challenge than the feeling that he or she will sink with it if it goes down, but reap none of the glory if things take a

turn for the better. Tell the people who are working for you what
the rules of the game are, as you see them. The more control you
can hand over – of people, time and resources – the better
motivated your problem-solver will be and the more likely it is that
a real personal commitment will be made, though you must also
provide support, such as regular meetings, to ensure the new
responsibilities do not become overwhelming. People are highly
motivated when they feel they are empowered, when they have
both control and responsibility. That is part of the reason why the
self-employed rarely seem to need days off sick. It also explains
why, under the Soviet system, productivity on the big collective
farms was abysmal, when the same peasants were able to wring
bumper crops out of the few square metres that each was allowed
to farm privately.

➡ ASK YOUR PEOPLE WHAT THEY NEED

Most people, after all, have a drive to succeed. Few enjoy failure.
You do not necessarily need to pile on new material incentives to
persuade people to stretch for success. You can ask the members of
your team what is needed to remove constraints on their performance and unleash their energy and they will frequently be able to
tell you. People's self-knowledge can be startling at times, so ask
them: 'What is inhibiting your own natural motivation to achieve
more?' The range of answers is potentially limitless, but there are
several that occur time and again: 'I feel helpless', 'I feel hopeless',
and 'I feel exhausted' are all familiar replies and are useful
reminders of the way mental, physical and motivational states are
often closely intertwined. With these people in particular, the next
question can be genuinely liberating. Try asking: 'What one
change would make your job more rewarding for you?' Sometimes
the changes suggested are alterations to tiny procedural matters
that have taken on grotesque significance and can be sorted out
almost instantly. Sometimes they are impractical changes, on a
scale that would count as business process re-engineering or that
would require a major reshuffling of the workforce. But the
answers to this question will almost always suggest ways forward

that would never have attracted the attention of someone whose starting point was your own perspective.

If you are trying to motivate people who are feeling stuck and helpless, it is more important than ever to break projects down into manageable stages, with clear and achievable interim goals. Feedback is strategically important because of its role in confirming that projects are still on the right track. But it is even more important from a motivational point of view, because it is part of the reward system that makes people feel good about themselves and what they are doing and encourages them to go on and do even more of it, even better.

Effective motivators pay attention to planning and structuring projects and workloads so that positive feedback loops reinforce the team's enthusiasm to succeed. These mechanisms can sometimes be purely monetary – sales campaigns can be structured with escalating commissions as predetermined thresholds are passed and subcontractors can be encouraged with payment schemes offering bonuses for early completion of project stages. But there are also the more intangible motivation factors. People can be strongly motivated with prompt and well-informed praise for their interim achievements at regular briefing meetings. Attending a meeting at which it is formally recognised that you have successfully met a deadline or passed a milestone is a rewarding and motivating experience in itself. The confirmation that you are right on course is part of the positive feedback and also validates the larger plan, offering reassurance that the approach has been right and that the strategy for reaching the big goals is viable. The process has a momentum of its own. Each step forward makes the next step easier. Each milestone passed shortens the perceived distance to the next one.

Putting these ideas into practice to motivate others is sometimes easier than convincing yourself they can be used to fire your own motivation. Yet the techniques for self-motivation are just the same – and they work just as well. Ask yourself the questions you ask your colleagues – 'What is inhibiting your own natural motivation?' and 'What one change would make your job more rewarding?' – and pay careful attention to the answers that emerge. Break long and complex projects down into small chunks, with built-in rewards wherever possible, to avoid being daunted by the mountain you have to climb. Choose goals and priorities carefully and use your memory and imagination to create the most vivid images and feelings of what success will be like. Mix towards and away from, carrot and stick, but remember pleasure is the inner measure of success and the carrot will ultimately take you further, once you are sure about where you are going.

In a Nutshell   Motivating

- **Make things compelling for yourself and others:**
  - Find two examples of things you achieved when highly motivated.
  - Is it easier to find them from the working part of your life or from outside work?
  - Did you move away from the unwanted, or towards what you wanted – or both?

- **A clear, bright vision of success is the best motivator:**
  - We draw on the past for sensory memories of how good we once felt.
  - People project into the future by recreating the past.
  - If the experience is strong, vivid and specific, the promise focuses our attention on achieving.
  - Relive the memories of how good it felt and what you could see, hear, smell and taste.

- **Motivating yourself is about building up the full emotional reality of a 'future memory':**
  - Pleasure is the payoff for succeeding, the internal yardstick of success.

- **If you know it would be good to make improvements and you don't, why not?**
  - Trying to motivate yourself to not smoke, not bite your nails or · not blame your parents is doomed.
  - You can't imagine negative concepts properly.

- *'Away from'* is generally associated with the 'pain' half of the pain/pleasure model.

- Beyond immediate danger and discomfort, it loses power fast.

• **Mix sticks and carrots for the best motivational cocktail, for yourself and others.**

• **Could you delegate your motivation?**

• **Prioritisation is a vital element in self-motivation:**

   - Whatever you pay attention to is what you have prioritised.

• **Four motivation myths:**

   - 'I am not a very motivated person.'

   - 'I don't have a lot of motivation.'

   - 'Motivation is all you need.'

   - 'You don't need motivation – just talk money.'

• **How much of what you don't want will make you happy?**

• **Human behaviour is fundamentally purposeful:**

   - People do things in order to try to achieve what matters to them.

   - Ask them to tell you what their aims are.

   - You cannot satisfy people with money.

   - We feel good if our work becomes part of us.

• **Let people know they'll get the credit if their work goes well:**

   - The more control you can hand over, with proper support, the more motivated your people will be.

   - Ask team members: 'What is inhibiting your own natural motivation to achieve more?'

• **Try asking: 'What one change would make your job more rewarding for you?'**

- **Break projects into manageable stages, with achievable interim goals:**
  - Feedback makes people feel good about themselves.
  - Plan projects and workloads so positive feedback loops reinforce enthusiasm.
  - Prompt praise for a deadline met or a milestone passed is motivating.

- **Ask yourself the questions you ask your colleagues:**
  - 'What is inhibiting your own natural motivation?'
  - 'What one change would make your job more rewarding?'
  - Break complex projects down into small chunks, with built-in rewards wherever possible.

- **Mix towards and away from, carrot and stick:**
  - Pleasure is the inner measure of success.
  - The carrot will take you further, once you know where you're going.

Chapter 6
Getting Your Own Way

'i have noticed that when chickens quit quarreling over their food they often find there is enough for all of them i wonder if it might not be the same way with the human race'

(Don Marquis, 1933)

➡ HOW TO GET WHAT YOU NEED, WHILE KEEPING PEOPLE ON YOUR SIDE

Most of us instinctively shy away from people who seem too selfish, too overpowering or too ruthless in pursuit of their own objectives. But it is often the way they go about it, rather than the goals they seek, that makes them offensive. You can't blame sales people for seeking to close a sale. You can certainly blame them for insulting your intelligence with a pushy manner and ill-thought-out arguments or for trying to sell you a garage when you don't have a car. In fact, getting your own way has always had an unjustifiably bad press, to the point where many children grow up half-convinced that it is automatically wrong. That is nonsense, of course. But it is not only children who need to be told. Many adults could do with a Post-it note on the corner of the desk or stuck to the bathroom mirror bearing the reassuring motto: 'It's OK to want to get your own way.'

The confusion is understandable, in a culture where the metaphors and model structures that influence our thinking come from fields like competitive sport or our adversarial legal system. If we are playing tennis or rugby or taking a case to court, we expect to see clear-cut winners and losers. One player or side comes out on top, while the other is left with none of the spoils. But life itself isn't always like that. There is nothing wrong with wanting to get your own way, most of the time, because your success will not necessarily be at anyone else's expense.

It is a serious mistake to assume that for you to achieve your goals other people must be done out of theirs. It is equally wrong-headed to assume that others do not want what you want. Many business problems and family disputes have no more substance to them than a set of assumptions like this.

Example

One of our clients told us how a wholesale company he does business with needed a 20-ton load moved from Glasgow to London overnight. Because it couldn't justify the cost of a heavy truck driving through the night, it didn't call our client, the haulage contractor. Unknown to the wholesalers, however, the haulier was just finalising a delivery in Stirling, 20 miles north of Glasgow. He was cursing the absence of a backload and the need to clock up over 400 non-revenue-earning miles bringing an empty vehicle home to London. If the wholesalers had dropped their assumptions and picked up the phone, that load could have come south for a bargain price of £50 or £60 and both companies would have been miles better off.

In the above example there was an unrecognised alignment of objectives between customer and supplier and a chance went begging, all for want of good communication. But what if your business partners knew that you did not make assumptions about their needs and would always follow through and keep checking? Suppose they knew you were good at recognising their objectives and finding ways to align your goals and theirs, so that they could get what they wanted if you achieved your aims? That would be a powerful incentive for close co-operation. It would give the people you deal with a reason to want to help you. It would make win–win arrangements something more than an elegant bit of management theory. And it would greatly increase the likelihood of being able to get your own way, without coercion, compromising your ideals or paying over the odds.

Some people can do it. Some individuals seem to have the knack of enlisting the willing co-operation of others with a minimum of fuss and effort. Some managers seem able to influence everyone around them to see the positive, constructive potential in situations, even when dealing with new colleagues, customers and suppliers. They make it seem easy. They are the people with a talent for building rapport and developing that rapport into good working relationships.

➡ THE SECRET OF INFLUENCE

Rapport is the key to more rewarding, pleasurable and efficient business relationships. It is the secret of influence, the only real alternative to brute force in many business situations. Whenever you want repeat business or simply need to work productively with people over a period of time, you are inevitably going to be involved in building and maintaining ongoing relationships. Otherwise you will be starting from scratch every time, reinventing the wheel over and over again, patching and fudging when things go wrong and always vulnerable to mishaps and misunderstandings.

The art of establishing rapid and durable rapport is definitely one of the 'soft' skills of management, but its results can manifest themselves in the bluntest and most hard-edged ways. Just try getting a few pallets of engineering spares unloaded from the back of a van without the co-operation of the one person in Goods Inwards authorised to drive the forklift. The spares may be urgently needed and you can be a head of department, chief engineer or even the MD, but if you face a campaign of passive resistance from disgruntled members of your own warehouse staff, you are going to find everything takes at least twice as long as it should.

There are some men and women whose ability to build rapport seems entirely natural and enviably spontaneous. It doesn't matter how much is truly inborn and how much comes from learning early on that life can be easier, sweeter and more fun if you get off on the right foot with people. They have that warmth and openness that strikes an answering spark in the most surly stranger. But the rest of us need to pay some attention to how the dynamics of individual relationships work, if we are to emulate their nonchalant ability to engage with people within seconds of meeting them for the first time.

A set of valuable techniques for improving our performance in this area has been developed and refined over the last 25 years in NLP. The basic skill is known as pacing and leading and its success is built upon the fact that every human being tends to feel more comfortable with others who are like him or her, rather than people who create the impression of being different, alien and potentially puzzling or threatening.

Most people operate from a mindset that says: 'Whatever I'm like, I know I'm normal. It follows that the less like me people are, the stranger and the more unpredictable they are likely to be. My clone and I might find life boring together, but at least we'd know there would be no dangerous surprises.' Pacing and leading means going out of your way to meet the other person on his or her home ground, to accept, for the moment, his or her model of the way the world works and to tune the way you are and the way you communicate to the wavelength he or she is on. That is not easy to do if you're certain your way of being is the right way and people who are different from you are just strange or stupid.

Just as people who are walking along together naturally fall into step with each other, people who are relaxed and in sympathy with each other tend to strike up an unconscious harmony. They may adopt similar postures, speak at the same volume and in similar tones and rhythms and use the same sort of expressions and gestures. If you watch them closely, with an eye for the rise and fall of their shoulders, you may even see that they have fallen into similar breathing patterns.

There is a delicate feedback system at work here, a system of fine-tuned messages and detailed adjustments and acknowledgements, that takes the principle of falling into step with each other a great deal further. This pacing happens entirely outside the realms of the participants' conscious awareness, but you can't miss the results. People come out of meetings saying things like 'I'm not sure how much we actually sorted out, but I know it'll be all right – he's someone I can work with.' Or they say 'Brilliant, she understands just what we need', or even 'Nice guy – couldn't shift him on the price, but we can live with that.' Whatever the immediate outcome, in business terms, the rapport that has been established

is an asset for all future contact between these people and the
starting point for a useful working relationship.

➡ DEALING WITH ANGER AND HOSTILITY

But what happens when you need to get your own way and
natural, spontaneous rapport is not on the agenda? How can you
defuse the situation when stubborn or bloody-minded people are
out to get you and determined not to be charmed by any
conciliatory words you come out with? That is when you need to
apply a little technical expertise. There are techniques that will let
you begin laying the foundations of rapport in the face of real
negativity, so that you can first pace the person in front of you and
then begin to lead him or her towards your idea of a reasonable
solution.

Let's take anger as a test case. Suppose you are feeling extremely
angry and, when you tell the relevant person, the response is just 'I
can see you're feeling very angry,' said in an oh-so-calm voice.
What effect does that soothing tone have on you? Does it soothe
you? Or does it incense you? Most people say it drives them nuts.
The reason is that they don't feel that what they are expressing is
really being acknowledged. As one person put it: 'Don't patronise
me with your "understanding".' In this kind of situation, you need
to know that you've been heard. Anger is energy and being angry is
a very energised state, so a super-calm response is a real mismatch.
You don't usually want the other person to just get angry back – at
any rate, not in customer service – but you need to know you are
being taken seriously. Part of the way people gauge this is by the
energy and tone and manner with which they're met. So a clear,
straight response that doesn't flinch and doesn't magically try to
smooth all the wrinkles away is probably going to be much more
effective. After all, which would you prefer?

Even when you meet outright hostility, the rules do not change.
Your antagonist will still feel more comfortable and less threatened
– and hence less aggressive – as he picks up subliminal signals that
you are less unlike him than he thought. Copying his ear-
scratching or other behavioural tics would undoubtedly win you a
punch in the mouth or a volley of abuse. But seeking to match

subtler aspects of his physical behaviour, and especially his energy level and language, is a shrewd and surprisingly fast-acting way of winding down the tension and disarming the situation.

Where behavioural matching is concerned, a little goes a long way. Mimicry is out. But you can slouch if he slouches, match his level of animation and excitement, use similar hand gestures and facial expressions and act in the same physical style – tense and reined-in or large and expansive – without any danger of being challenged. At the same time as you are doing this physical pacing, you should be trying to see the world through his eyes so that you can start to get in step with the values that lie behind his attitudes.

Your aim should be to find out what is important to the other person and to work out how matters can be arranged so that getting what you want can also help your opposite number get what he or she wants. You are pacing the person and trying to establish rapport so that you can then, ideally, lead on towards a mutually advantageous resolution of your differences. But the world is not always an ideal place. Sometimes it becomes clear that your business needs are genuinely incompatible. If this seems to be the case, take a little more time to check from every angle you can think of and see whether you can identify any common ground at all, or any overlap of interest on which you might build.

If the answer is no, you are faced with some tough choices. You need to take stock of the situation and ask yourself two more questions: 'How crucial is this deal, this person or this organisation to our future?' and 'Is it worth stalling for a day, or a week, and hoping that time might alter any significant factors in my favour?' Time is a much-underrated agent of change. It was Prime Minister Harold Wilson who observed that 'a week is a long time in politics'. But it is not just the political world that moves on. Often people's positions are influenced by unforeseen factors. Never assume that because the answer is no this week, it will be no next week, still less next month.

But if time is not on your side and the deal and the person are vitally important, getting your own way is going to need you to improvise a new approach to suit the precise circumstances. This will mean having the flexibility to do whatever it takes, which may be a far cry from what you would normally choose to do.

➡ FLEXIBILITY MEANS NEVER BEING STUCK FOR AN IDEA

Flexibility is a much underrated factor in business circles, where the impression is sometimes given that determination and iron-willed intransigence are the main qualities needed for success. Yet it is no coincidence that all the oriental martial arts, for example, are designed to teach their followers to win through flexibility, rather than sheer strength. Judo, karate, kung fu, tae kwon do and aikido all recognise that people are creatures of habit and that their habits make them rigid. The strong but rigid warrior has fewer choices when reacting to a situation, leaving him vulnerable to someone who is more flexible. Showing flexibility in this kind of business context means introducing unexpected change, destabilising established positions and provoking a reassessment of what is being discussed.

Example

A past master of this way of thinking is Carlton H. Sheets, an American real estate dealer who has made a career out of buying property with no money down – and teaching others how to do the same thing. Watching his methods is a fascinating experience, for several reasons. First, he is very clear that the deal should never be laden with emotion (how does that compare with the roller coaster of feelings you experience each time you move house?). Second, he will come up with one suggestion after another in negotiating with the seller. If one no-money-down proposal doesn't work, he just offers an alternative deal. Third, he is always looking for new ways to creatively finance real estate purchases. Sometimes his students have even been able to buy property with no deposit and receive several thousand dollars in cash on completion of the deal.

So if you are negotiating a contract, jump outside the box and ask yourself what other ways of achieving this outcome there might be. What else could be factored into – or taken out of – the deal? Consider how you might change its scope. Suggest that a year's maintenance is bundled in with the product. Say that you want a price excluding software, because you can source that elsewhere. Explain that you could pay more if you were offered world rights, instead of just the US and Europe. Rather than argue about how the cake should be cut, bake a bigger cake. There may well be a point, somewhere along the line, where both sides suddenly realise they can see a profit in coming to a deal.

The other issue involved in getting your own way is that often you can only get it with someone else's active co-operation. If you ask people the blunt question 'Are you getting what you want?' – at home or at work – the reply is frequently 'No, but if only X would do Y, everything would be great.' This is a bad sign. Being in a situation where you wait for X to get round to wanting to do Y before you can have what you want is inherently disempowering. The first step towards a remedy is to recognise that this kind of waiting corrodes the soul. Doing is better, even if you don't succeed immediately.

Ask X, as directly, plainly and frankly as you can, to give you what you need. Although this may be a vital subject for you, it may not have crossed X's mind that it would matter to you, or that there is even an issue there at all. You may get your own way immediately. But even if X is deliberately withholding co-operation, you are already making progress, because you will now know, rather than having to indulge in mindreading. There are also two non-solutions people frequently resort to. First, you might consider trying to force X to help you. But coercion makes enemies and breeds grudges. It is fundamentally inefficient, especially over the longer term, because people walk away. Second, if you rule out force, you might think about using manipulation to get your own way. However the problem with manipulating people is that you produce a situation where X feels good now, but will feel conned at some later date. You have lost a potential ally and found a procedure for creating enemies with long memories and plenty of stamina. And some of them will be just biding their time. You end up feeling as if you are living life on the run. Your self-esteem is undermined, and once that goes the range of things that it is possible for you to achieve is also seriously undermined. Living like this is not exactly stress-free either. The more you do it, the more you have to find new contacts. As doors keep closing, you feel more and more disconnected, alienated and excluded. At the extreme, this is the mindset of the criminal.

➡ MAKING X WANT TO DO Y: THE ALGEBRA OF SUCCESS

In the long run, you are far better off dismissing coercion and manipulation as means to your ends and relying on changing X's mind by using the skills you already have and acquiring the influencing skills that are so easy to learn with NLP. If your straightforward request has been refused, your next step is to ask yourself: 'What do I need to do to make X want to do Y?' This is a powerful way of looking at the situation, because it presupposes that you will be able to find some profit or payoff that draws X towards wishing to help you get your own way. In business, these payoffs can be couched in financial terms or in terms of reciprocal favours between departments and individuals.

Example

In one company we worked with, the accounts department was being driven to distraction because people in Sales would not complete their post-sale paperwork either properly or on time. Applying the 'What do I need to do to make X want to do Y?' formula revealed the opportunity for a simple, self-regulating solution. A minor adjustment was made to the system, so that the payment of sales bonuses was automatically triggered by the arrival of completed paperwork in Accounts, rather than being calculated from records kept in Sales. It took no time at all for the sales force to realise that money came through faster under the new system. The 'bad habits' of an energetic and hardworking sales team underwent a miraculous overnight cure and the previous chaos was replaced by a steady flow of impeccably completed documentation.

In a Nutshell　Getting Your Own Way

- **Get what you need, while keeping people on your side:**
  - Remind yourself: 'It's OK to want to get your own way.'
  - Your success won't necessarily be at anyone else's expense.
  - Don't assume others don't want what you want.
  - If you're good at recognising people's aims and aligning yours

and theirs, they'll want to be helpful.

- **Rapport is the key to better business relationships:**
  - The basic skill is known as 'pacing and leading'.
  - People feel more comfortable with others when they feel they have something in common.

- **Pacing and leading means going out of your way to meet people on their home ground:**
  - When people are in rapport, there's unconscious harmony.
  - Similar volume, voice tone and rhythms and use of similar expressions and gestures.
  - Anger is energy
  - People need to know they are being taken seriously.
  - A clear, straight response that doesn't flinch will be the most effective.
  - Mimicry is not matching.

- **Match posture, animation, gestures, expression and physical style – tense and tight or expansive.**

- **See the world through the other person's eyes to get in step with his or her values:**
  - Find out what is important to the other person.
  - Ideally, getting what you want can help your opposite number succeed, too.
  - Look for any common ground at all, or overlap of interest you can build on.

- **Never assume that no this week means no next week, still less next month:**
  - Ask: 'How crucial is this deal, this person or this organisation to our future?'
  - Think, 'Is it worth holding off for a day, or a week, and hoping time might alter any significant factors?'

- **Flexibility means introducing change, destabilising positions and provoking reassessments:**
  - Come up with different suggestions.
  - If the first no-deposit proposal doesn't work, the property dealer always offers an alternative.
  - When negotiating a contract, jump outside the box.
  - Ask yourself what the other ways of achieving this outcome might be.
  - What else could be factored into – or taken out of – the deal?

- **Waiting for X to do Y so you can have what you want is disempowering:**
  - Ask X to give you what you need.
  - It may not have crossed X's mind that it would matter to you.
  - Force and manipulation are unproductive strategies.
  - You'll do better using the influencing skills that are easy to learn with NLP.

- **Use algebra: 'What do I need to do to make X want to do Y?'**
  - Used creatively, this formula can often lead to simple, self-regulating solutions.

Chapter 7
Giving Feedback, Taking Criticism

'Great fleas have little fleas upon their backs to bite 'em. And little fleas have lesser fleas and so *ad infinitum*.'

(Augustus De Morgan, 1850)

➡ HOW TO MAKE FEEDBACK WORK FOR YOU

Let's start this important chapter with the simple facts of the case. What you give to your people is invaluable and constructive feedback that will help them modify and improve their performance. What you get in your own appraisal, when the boot's on the other foot, is ill-considered and vindictive criticism that ignores the evidence of your achievement and totally fails to recognise the validity of your contribution. Funny, that. Isn't it strange that the assessment you are offering should be so objective and free from emotional loading, while that which is offered to you can seem like an assault on your very being?

If this is the day of your half-yearly work review and appraisal, your line manager may go home at the end of the afternoon and spend a few minutes this evening thinking about the three or four people he or she has to put through this process tomorrow. You will drive home like a maniac, kick the cat and be in need of several drinks before you take your jacket off.

This, unfortunately, is not all parody. It is all too close to what happens every week of the year, all over the country. Otherwise competent bosses, facing a company requirement to conduct appraisal and feedback sessions at regular intervals, call their staff in one by one and deliver a blunderbuss volley of criticisms, advice, praise, hearsay and personal observation that often fails to produce any kind of purposeful result. Wh it is even worse is that however high you rise in the business world, unless you sit in solitary splendour on top of the pile as chairman, MD or CEO, you will probably be on the receiving end of much the same sort of treatment throughout your career. And the degree of competence with which it is carried out seldom improves substantially as you scale the corporate pyramid.

➡ FEEDBACK ON FEEDBACK

It is all done in the name of feedback. But the feedback on the efficacy of feedback sessions is very negative already – and getting worse, as the results begin to come in from a range of academic research projects, including one disturbing study on learning from failure run by London Business School's Centre for Organisational Research.

The ability of human beings to sort for assaults on ego and self-esteem should never be underestimated. While the manager nurses the fond hope of having given a fair and balanced picture, the recipient of this coolly symmetrical appraisal feels threatened, defensive, unappreciated and destabilised. The problem is that the 'exchange rate' that exists between positive and negative feedback units is about nine or ten to one.

As the London Business School study highlights, the brain will discount large quantities of positive information, especially if any of the negative feedback is perceived to be an attack on the person at the identity level. This is why approaches like the popular 'feedback sandwich' may not be as effective as their advocates would like to hope. With the feedback sandwich, you begin with positive, confidence-building praise for the best aspects of your subordinate's performance, then feed back the more critical observations and talk about how improvements can be made and finally round off with more positive feedback. But if the positive feedback is just about the person's behaviour and the negative is taken at the level of identity, guess which message stays with the listener. The 'victim' leaves the room, closes the door and mutters: 'All that window dressing and that imbecile thinks I didn't notice what was going on when I was being attacked.' As a result, the feedback sandwich may not work as well as you thought it should, because the bread is largely ignored and the filling is regarded with fear and suspicion.

Criticism hurts, feedback helps. In the end the only definitions that matter are the ones that work in the real world. If it hurts you – however well it was intended – what you're getting is criticism. If it helps, it's feedback. In NLP, there is a useful way of looking at things that don't go right, encapsulated in the slogan 'There is no failure, only feedback'. On one level, that may sound like wishful thinking and an inaccurate reflection of the way things really are. But the point about this formulation is that it is a tool, not a truth. There are arguably many cases where failure seems to exist in clear and palpable forms. But if you work from the presupposition, true or not, that 'there is no failure, only feedback', you will start dealing with any set of circumstances much more proactively.

Every response or lack of response you pick up when you communicate with the world is feedback of some sort. There is always useful information to be gleaned from it, though it may not be the kind of information you are expecting. If you give a business presentation with plenty of strong ideas and it fails to go down as well as you hoped, that is feedback. It doesn't necessarily mean there is anything wrong with you, your ideas or your presentation style, though. You may be receiving feedback about other circumstances and constraints affecting your audience that are not public knowledge yet. If the people in your audience have just heard that their division is being sold off, or that the field sales manager has just had a heart attack, or that a row has broken out in the press about the safety of their products, their reactions to your arguments will be understandably muted. You cannot always guess what is going on. What you can do is notice that the response is not what you expected and start to be curious and alert for clues as to what the explanation might be.

➡ YOU HAVE TO GO WRONG TO GO FORWARD

If you are going to road-test the 'there is no failure, only feedback' presupposition, it is a fair question to ask 'What is a failure?' Since our entire development, from the first weeks of life onwards, is based on trial and error learning, where does the concept of failure fit in? An error is not a failure. It can't be, even though most people confuse the two. If trial and error is the route to progress – and it applies to an Edison, an Einstein or a Hawking, just as much as to a toddler who is learning to walk – then the error part of the process can't just be missed out or dismissed as failure. You have to go wrong to go forward. So the question is not 'Why am I not perfect?'; it is 'What am I going to learn from this error?'

As soon as you start to learn from a mistake, you begin to get a payoff for the future. In scientific research, for example, 'failure' is both routine and respectable. To learn that a hypothesis is incorrect may well yield valuable information about where to go next and where not to invest further resources. In professional sport, too, learning from mistakes and defeat is normal and assimilated into the process of moving on towards success. Whatever disappointment is associated with disproving a pet hypothesis or failing to win a football match or a golf tournament, there is little sentimental lingering in the past. The emotional pain is left behind as soon as possible. Attention is quickly focused forward, onto learning from the experience and constructive planning to achieve better results. The contrast with some businesses we have worked with is stark. There is no long wait for a formal quarterly or half-yearly appraisal, at which the ghosts of failures will be summoned up to be chewed over again. There is shared acceptance that not every theory will bear fruit and that no team can win every match or even play well every time. And there is a general, realistic understanding that associating fear and anxiety with failure is simply not appropriate. Sports people and scientists expect to fail sometimes. They are rewarded for their best contributions and peak achievements, rather than for a low level of error-free consistency.

If you are setting out to pick up all the helpful feedback that is available to you, it is clear that you should be on the lookout all the time. Feedback is not a twice-a-year thing that surfaces only when the calendar says it is appraisal week. If you waited for the formal sessions, you would have missed half the game. Ideally, of course, you would be so clear about what was going on around you that you would know in advance what the outcome of your next appraisal would be.

As a step towards this kind of omniscience, try to predict what will happen when you next have to go through a formal appraisal.

This is not a parlour game. It is a valuable exercise, because it edges you round towards looking at the situation from your manager's point of view. Once you have done it, you'll have useful information about what to expect. And it will be all the more surprising to find that you are able to identify several aspects of your strengths and weaknesses that your manager does not appear to notice. These omissions matter, because the differences between what you would discuss and what your manager chooses to pick out show how realistic the management's view of your potential is. If your good points are being ignored and your weaknesses are hauled to the fore, you need to make a conscious effort to steer the discussion into areas where things you have done implicitly bear witness to your strengths and versatility.

Given that feedback is a most precious commodity and the basis of all learning, the opportunity to give constructive one-to-one feedback to the people you work with should be something every manager welcomes. Yet, for many managers, giving feedback is a source of great unease. They put off feedback sessions until they are obliged to do them and then go through the motions, uncomfortable that they are not properly equipped to make them as effective and valid as they should be.

➡ THE DOS AND DON'TS OF FEEDBACK

This is not a promising starting point. But it suggests that we should take a purely practical approach and try to pinpoint specific ways in which future appraisal and feedback sessions can be made more productive, simply by doing some things and avoiding doing others.

Let's start with the nightmare scenario. This is how *not* to give feedback about unsatisfactory work.

How not to give feedback
- just launch in – attack, right from the start, with no preamble

- make your complaints unjust and ambiguous, so it's not clear what should be done
- blame the individual for group failures
- fail to invite comment
- regard all responses as time-wasting excuses
- generalise, with no facts and no specific examples
- target attitudes, rather than performance
- make unverifiable accusations; this ensures that what you allege is also unfalsifiable.

The impact of this kind of feedback is profoundly debilitating, at the level of one's personal identity. It also does the manager no good; he or she will be seen as either hugely incompetent, unimaginative and insensitive, or motivated by malice. Criticism of this sort is the perfect vehicle for expressing hostility. Yet the key factor – the use of unjust, unspecific and unverifiable accusations – often surfaces in a diluted form as nothing more than a symptom of inexperience.

The less factual content the 'feedback' embodies, the harder the criticisms are to refute.

Example

In the old days of the Fleet Street newspapers, it was common practice for autocratic editors wanting to give their senior staff a dressing down to accuse them of being 'unprofessional'. All journalists share a sense of vocation and pretensions to professionalism, whether they work for the red-top tabloids or the broadsheets, so that in itself was a well-aimed blow to the ego. But 'unprofessionalism' was such an intangible charge that it was impossible to disprove. Even leathery old hacks would carry the memory of the insult around with them, feeling it rankle under the skin and wondering, in their darkest hours, whether it just might be true.

Giving good feedback is the very opposite of the nightmare scenario. It takes account of the fact that most people approach the idea of feedback, in the work context, feeling apprehensive and defensive. Many assume feedback is going to mean criticism – and that if it is needed, their performance must have been found wanting. Good feedback is based on an understanding that the intention is positive and that the best possible outcome is an improvement in performance, coupled with a strengthening of the working relationship.

➡ SEPARATE BEHAVIOUR FROM IDENTITY

Good feedback begins by clearly differentiating a person's identity from his or her behaviour. Feedback should be about actions, about what you do, not who you are. It is an important distinction, but one that is frequently blurred in everyday life. Listen to people at parties. 'What do you do?' someone asks. 'Oh, I'm a pilot/plumber/software engineer/PA/teacher/farmer,' is the reply, more often than not. Logically speaking, the answer to the question should have been: 'I fly planes/mend pipes/fix bugs/carry the can for someone on three times my salary/teach/farm.' We define ourselves so often by what we do that we come to believe that that is what we are. And it's not necessarily a problem. But it certainly explains why losing one's job or suffering a forced change of job status can feel so deeply threatening. If people are what they do, if their existence is defined by their work activity, what happens to their identity if they are made redundant?

The art of separating behaviour from identity is an important life skill for use at home, with partners, in-laws and children, as well as in feedback sessions at work. And it is hardly a new idea. 'Hate the sin, but love the sinner' was advocated by Saint Paul two thousand years ago. It is certainly the first step in taking the heat out of all kinds of conflicts, opening up the possibility of two people looking back together on a past event and viewing it without having to peer through swirling clouds of guilt or anger. Feedback is information for the future. But to make the most of it, both parties have to be able to disengage from the clutter of the immediate past. What has already been done can't be undone, though even those who feel responsible for and embarrassed by mistakes often find it hard to leave the emotional echoes of yesterday's errors behind them. To encourage this detachment and point the session firmly towards the future is an essential part of the scene-setting task for the manager in a feedback session.

Once it has been convincingly established that the feedback you have in mind is constructive, two-way and concerned with actions and objectives, rather than personalities, you should be able to move ahead in an atmosphere of reasonable trust.

Remembering to shun the kind of unspecific and unverifiable criticisms highlighted in the nightmare scenario, you need to provide your staff member with clear examples of what he or she has been doing right, what has been done incorrectly and what needs to be changed for the better. The emphasis should be on outcomes: what can be seen to work and what demonstrably fails to produce the required results. There is a catch here, though, that you should be aware of. The wider, longer-term consequences of this person's actions may be made visible to you, possibly because of feedback you pick up from other departments, but not to him or her. If you take this opporunity to explain what you can see from your level, how it fits into the broader perspective and why it matters to you, this will help to dispel any impression that you are judging the work by purely private or arbitrary standards. Giving feedback is partly a form of teaching, and this is your opportunity to teach your people to see the bigger picture.

Part of your job as a manager is to put forward well-chosen examples of how performance levels can be improved, so suggestions about how a situation with clients could be handled or specific advice on how to implement technical procedures more effectively are obviously important. But you can also offer a little more, by drawing attention to examples of good practice or even useful and positive attitudes among other members of staff. 'Watch the way Susan goes about finding what the customer really wants' is a sensible way to encourage the passing on of detailed skills developed from the experience of senior staff and probably never written down anywhere. Just as the traditional craft apprentice learnt his trade by watching and working with a master craftsman, until he was so familiar with the tools and materials that he could eventually step into his master's shoes, so there is lot to be gained from the study and emulation of success. 'Everyone on the board likes the fact that Sam's ideas are always backed up with proper figures' is a different, but equally useful, version of the same technique – a specific way of indicating how one aspect of the job could be done better, by offering a role model. You could also suggest the person could talk to Sam about how the figures can be compiled.

➡ DON'T TAKE IT PERSONALLY

Almost nobody in business is guaranteed safe from the curse of incompetent feedback. So it is important, when your turn comes to be in the firing line, to have some techniques for making the best of the situation. You will encounter incompetently delivered feedback at some stage. It may feel like personal criticism. So how are you going to avoid feeling crushed? And how are you going to get something positive out of it?

The trick of taking hostile and ill-directed criticism like this and coming up smiling is not to take it personally, *especially* if you can see that it was meant in a very personal way. If you take it personally, you get dragged in. Your identity is on the line and you have to defend it. And defending your identity is serious, a survival issue. It is by embroiling senior managers in messy, personal arguments like this, where they will eventually defend their identity by saying 'Stick your job, I'm going' that large and ruthless companies sometimes offload people whose faces don't fit. So don't get drawn.

The second trick to get you through is to disarm any but the most rabid criticism by genuinely accepting it as useful feedback, even if it is malevolently intended. Listen for the detail, so that you really do know what the other person is talking about (and bear in mind that there may be more than one person involved, on the other side of the table, and that no two people ever think exactly alike). The point is to identify any grain of truth in the other side's observations and then let your critic see, unmistakably, that you have taken on board the valid points that were being made. This may well wrongfoot your interlocutor, because suddenly there is no need – or justification – for pushing hard to drive the points home.

The third survival trick, if you really are under attack, is to focus ferociously on analysing the situation and thinking: 'How can I make this work for me, so that I never have to hear this sort of poison from anyone ever again?' Try to sort through the incoming fire and pluck out the bits that contain information that could be useful to you. If you feel too emotional and your rising emotion is not appropriate, ask yourself: 'What are these people trying to get at? Do I know what is driving this criticism?' Thinking in these analytical terms will blunt the impact of the assault and cause you to become a little dissociated from the immediacy of the situation. If you are good at dissociating yourself from your surroundings, you might even try to stand right outside the action and watch the scene that's developing, with you in the middle of it, from a disembodied fly-on-the-wall perspective.

➡ LEARN FROM YOUR EXPERIENCE

Whether or not you can manage to do this distancing, fly-on-the-wall act at the time, you will probably find you are quite capable of looking back on your mental movie of the experience afterwards. This is much easier and it is a good way of turning it to some use and panning some gold from the dirt. See the situation again but this time from outside, so that you can observe yourself as if you were watching a video of you in that experience. See yourself and how you reacted and how the other person behaved, in as much detail as you can muster, and look for the positive learning to be gained from the whole episode. Ask yourself, too: 'What can I learn about the way this feedback was delivered to me, to make sure that I never do this to anyone else?'

Look for the ways your experience can help you become a better manager. Learn from it what not to do and, by contrast, what you should be ready to do when you are giving feedback. Make a list of the dos and don'ts. If you look at the dos and realise that you know what should be done but don't know how to go about it, you should start thinking about what sort of training could help you plug the gaps. Perhaps there is a formal training course that would be useful. It might be possible to have a few well-focused sessions of executive coaching. Even talking to and spending time with people who you know can do this sort of thing well – learning by contagion – can be effective. The combination of tips and general attitudes that you can pick up via this route means that quite subtle aspects of their skills and approach may rub off on you.

Before leaving the subject of feedback, we would also invite you to consider how it fits into a more general methodology of management. One reason for making feedback sessions part of the regular routine is that there is merit in catching problems early. But some management styles work against this. Management by exception, for example, has its advantages. But one potential disadvantage is that managers only start to notice what is not going right when it actively goes wrong.

Feedback is the basis of learning and decision making. Poor feedback is the basis of poor learning – the child hears 'You stupid girl' and learns to be just that. Poor feedback produces poor decisions – poor market research results in a product for which there is no market. But there is another dimension to feedback and that's to start noticing what is working. A healthy antidote to the habit of noticing what's not working is to institute a regular stocktaking check-up, including yourself, first, and then your team, that asks: 'What are we doing that is working and what are we doing that isn't? What is working now that may not work so well in three or six or nine months' time?'

Feedback – proper, well-intentioned, sensibly delivered feedback, with a realistic two-way flow of information – is one of the main vehicles for quelling fear and superstition in times of uncertainty and for letting people know what they are doing right. Handled properly, it can build loyalty and boost performance, forestall future problems and inspire greater effort. It is an important tool for all managers and absolutely indispensable for those whose job involves steering people through rapid and unpredictable change.

In a Nutshell   **Giving Feedback, Taking Criticism**

- **Make feedback work for you.**

- **The feedback on feedback:**
  - Research shows reactions to appraisal session feedback are often negative.

- People discount positive comments, especially if the negatives seem like an attack at the identity level.
- A carefully balanced picture still leaves the recipient feeling threatened.
- The 'feedback sandwich' isn't always effective.
- Criticism hurts, feedback helps.

- **'There is no failure, only feedback.'**
  - Notice if the response is not what you expected, be curious and look for clues to explain why.

- **You have to go wrong to go forward:**
  - What are you going to learn from this error?
  - As soon as you start to learn from a mistake, you begin to get a payoff for the future.
  - In research and professional sport, lessons from defeat are assimilated as part of moving on to success.
  - Sports people and scientists expect to fail sometimes.
  - They are rewarded for peak achievements, not a low level of error-free consistency.

- **Try to predict what will happen when you next go through a formal appraisal:**
  - Put yourself in your manager's shoes.
  - Do differences between your concerns and your manager's show a realistic view of you?
  - If your good points are being ignored, steer the discussion towards positive evidence.

- **The dos and don'ts of feedback:**
  - Learn from the nightmare scenario.
  - Unjust, unspecific criticisms and unverifiable accusations are often just a symptom of inexperience.
  - Good feedback is based on an understanding that the intention is positive.

- The best possible outcome is improved performance and a strengthened working relationship.

- **Separate behaviour from identity:**
  - Feedback should be about what you do, not who you are.
  - Pointing the session firmly towards the future is part of the scene-setting task for the manager.
  - Give clear examples of what's going right, what has been done incorrectly and what needs improving.

- **Emphasise outcomes – what can be seen to work and what clearly fails to produce results:**
  - Explain what you can see from your level and how it fits into the broader perspective.
  - Draw attention to examples of good practice or useful attitudes.
  - Indicate how aspects of the job could be done better by offering role models.

- **Don't take it personally:**
  - Nobody in business is guaranteed safe from incompetent feedback.
  - Don't get drawn in.
  - Try genuinely accepting the criticism as useful feedback, even if it is malevolently intended.
  - Let your critic see, unmistakably, that you have taken on board the valid points.
  - Ask yourself: 'How can I make this work for me?'
  - Try standing right outside the action and watching from a fly-on-the-wall perspective.

- **Learn from your experience:**
  - Look back on your mental movie of the experience.
  - If you know what should be done but don't know how, think about training to help you plug the gaps.

- Spend time with people who can do this sort of thing well.
- Management by exception can mean only noticing what isn't going right when it actively goes wrong.
- Start regular stocktaking check-ups: what works, what doesn't and what may not work in the future?

Chapter 8
Resource Management

'The strongest principle of growth lies in human choice.'

(George Eliot, 1876)

➡ HOW TO MARSHAL YOUR OWN TIME AND TALENTS

What is it that makes a problem at work something you can surmount and take in your stride? What is it that makes another outwardly similar problem seem daunting, perplexing and ultimately overwhelming? The difference frequently has nothing to do with the facts of the case and the complexity of the issues, but everything to do with how you are feeling at the time.

Imagine trying to take all your major life decisions in the state you were in when you last had flu. Never mind the aching limbs and the feverish temperature, just think about what your view of the world was like at that particular time. Were you at your most resourceful? Was your natural zest for life tempered by a touch of defeatism? Would you admit that your judgement was a little impaired? It hardly needs saying that you are not at your best when you are fighting the flu bug. But a bout of flu is not generically different from many of the other distractions and depletions we suffer from time to time. Even being hungry, or feeling angry or tired, can produce a more modest version of the same debilitating effect. And, as with the flu, the results are not purely physical. Your internal state dictates what you can and can't focus on, face up to and do. It determines how resourceful and imaginative you can be in your thinking and how strong and energetic you can be in your actions.

Many people are surprised to learn that there is actually some scientific basis for the worker's traditional dislike of Monday mornings, quite apart from the contrast with the relaxation of the previous day. In fact, any morning is likely to be a bad time to cope with subjectively distressing events. Volunteers who submitted themselves to an experiment in which they were given regulated electric shocks (through their teeth!) at different times of day and night were asked to report how much pain they felt each time.

Objectively, nothing changed from one shock to the next. But the guinea pigs reported the pain as feeling almost twice as bad at certain times of the day, especially in the morning. In the early afternoon, after they had had lunch, the pain was not felt so severely. The response to pain is very personal and subjective, and, as always, there will have been many different factors working to define the state of each of the volunteers at different times of day. After all, no two people can ever enjoy precisely the same state, in every respect, any more than they can enjoy precisely the same personality. But in this case, the daily cycle of sensitivity and relative desensitisation reported by the volunteers was consistent and statistically significant, and further research is now going on to find out how universal the phenomenon is. Whatever contributions other elements were making to each volunteer's state, there was clearly one major component that was influencing them all in the same direction at the same hour.

For many office and factory workers, there is a point each day when they are aware that they are holding on by their fingertips. If you are sitting in an office trying to write a sales report on your PC, you are probably in no physical danger. You might end up with POIUYTREWQ embossed across your forehead from falling asleep over the keyboard, but no permanent damage will be done. If you are a taxi driver, a crane operator, an air traffic controller or a surgeon, it is obvious that actually nodding off carries the threat of potentially catastrophic consequences. But we are not primarily concerned, here, with people falling asleep at the wheel. We want to focus on the much more common and less spectacular cases. Many people routinely spend substantial parts of their day in an unresourceful state that means they are working at much less than their full capacity.

➡ ENERGY TO BURN

There is an energy crisis in most people's lives today. We feel tired too much of the time, without ever getting round to finding out why. We don't think of energy as being the key personal resource it is. We do not know what would be needed to maximise, conserve and increase our energy and we regard lack of energy as being something we cannot control and cannot act to change. Yet most of us know perfectly well that we don't get enough sleep.

If you need an alarm clock to wake you up every morning, that is feedback that you should not ignore. Research at Loughborough University shows that British adults average a little over seven hours sleep a night. But when psychiatrists at the US National Institute of Mental Health shut a group of volunteers in the dark for 14 hours each night for a month, the subjects fell into natural sleep patterns which settled at around eight and a quarter hours per night. Your brain and body need sleep for mental and physical reasons, to carry out a huge amount of filing and housekeeping and unconscious processing of information and to enable the immune system to do its work. The brain even steps up the rate at which it produces proteins while we are sleeping. If it's the alarm that jolts you awake every day, it is fair to assume that you are being woken prematurely and that some of these important processes may be left unfinished. If you haul yourself out of bed, weary and groggy, and have to zap your system with caffeine to kick-start your day, you are already showing signs of a fairly heavy-handed approach to the management of your personal energy resources. We all know people who go on from this sort of start to spend their working days lurching from one extreme to another, from mania to partial exhaustion and back, pushing themselves on from one hour to the next with coffee, cigarettes, chocolate, alcohol or even ritualised outbursts of anger (anger can be very energising, in the short term). This is poor resource management. It hardly adds up to being in control. It does not get more done and it does nothing for the quality of a person's output. If the answer is simply to be more realistic about the amount of sleeping time the individual needs, that is surely a change worth making.

There is certainly a more direct linkage than most people realise between the brain and the body, when it comes to storing and using energy. Our supply of physical energy comes from combustion processes that bring together carbohydrates from our food and oxygen from the air we breathe. The basic reaction produces carbon dioxide, water and heat energy. But we do not need the energy all at once. Some is used up immediately, but the rest is stored by the body, through the production of a chemical called ATP, or adenosine triphosphate. By manufacturing ATP, which can be broken down instantly to release energy when it is needed, the body is able to bank its reserves of energy until they are called for. And the organ that demands the largest share of these energy resources is the brain – three pounds or so of squishy meat that can burn fuel at ten times the rate of our other body tissues. Even when you lie down quietly, your brain is hogging one-fifth of your total energy supply, despite accounting for only about one-fortieth of your body weight. In cases of extreme sleep deprivation, the temperature control and energy banking processes go haywire and energy is burned off instead of being stored. Some rather drastic laboratory experiments with sleep-deprived rats have shown that this prompts them to eat furiously to try to maintain their energy reserves, and eventually, when this strategy no longer works, leads to total exhaustion and death.

➡ GET UP AND DO SOMETHING

To survive happy and healthy, we need to manage both sleeping patterns and energy levels as part of the broader goal of getting the most out of life. For many of us, the quickest route to tangible improvements on both fronts is to get out from behind our desks and steering wheels and start doing some physical exercise. The payoffs are enormous and easily won, while the amount of time, commitment and effort you put in is entirely under your own control. Regular aerobic exercise or sporting activity, several times a week, is the ideal and will lead directly to increased oxygenation of the blood, greater stamina and endurance and, less obviously, a marked improvement in your ability to concentrate. It is also an excellent way of changing your state, as your skin and your body will feel different for the rest of the day, and is often a straightforward solution for people in stress-filled jobs who are tormented by the inability to wind down and get to sleep at night. Yoga, t'ai chi, the Alexander technique and walking the dog are also worth considering, for there is only one rule: Do something.

The more energetic your new activity, the more spectacular the results are likely to be. But the very fact of starting to do something positive in relation to your own well-being is good for you in itself, both for its effect on your body and for the empowering sense of actively being in control of this aspect of your life. There are always conflicting claims on your time and other people's priorities to consider, to the point where it is easy to slip into the habit of putting yourself last. Making a commitment to yourself and setting aside time to do whatever activity you have chosen to do is a signal that you are taking responsibility for your well-being.

This element of taking control of aspects of your life and work is much more important than it seems. Stress is a major killer these days and there are increasing numbers of jobs that have obvious stress factors built in. New call centres for customer service operations are being opened every month. They employ many thousands of people, who necessarily spend all day every day dealing with worried or irate customers for whom things have gone wrong. Very few people ring customer helplines to express their delight with a product or service. So almost all these call centre staff have to live with a permanent barrage of negativity. Human beings are creatures of habit and we can become habituated to a level of stress that would once have been quite unacceptable to us. Then it becomes the norm and we only really notice what is even more stressful. The danger is that the baseline keeps being ratcheted up. Call centre customer service people have told us you just have to get used to it. It's as if their only way to survive is to allow themselves to become habituated to the high level of stress, which then becomes the baseline of 'normality'. When a faulty product is launched or the Christmas rush means unhappy customers have to wait to get through, the bombardment becomes more intense and the stress levels rise again, causing great discomfort until the emotional baseline is adjusted upwards once more.

It is not surprising that people in such jobs may come home in the evening and feel they need a couple of glasses of wine 'just to unwind'. After a while, it may be three glasses, and then a bottle.

This is part of a less than ideal stress 'management' programme – not necessarily what the experts would recommend, but an understandable antidote to the pressures of the working day. But that nightly bottle of wine is not, of course, limited to people working in call centres. There are a lot of stressful jobs and a lot of stressed people out there, from GPs and farmers to production managers, maintenance engineers, telesales workers, traffic wardens, probation officers and futures traders. It is quite possible to be overtaken by a rising tide of stress without realising what is happening until you have a major problem.

➡ HOW DO YOU HANDLE YOUR STRESS?

Ask yourself whether you are aware of the stress you face at work. Have you adjusted and habituated yourself, so that you no longer notice the toll it is taking? Everyone has to work out ways to deal with some work-related stress, but not everyone is aware of how he or she is doing it. Ask yourself: 'What does my personal stress management programme involve?' You may be one of the 'I cope as best I can' school. You may work out your frustrations in ferociously competitive games of squash. You may, if you are honest with yourself, recognise that you have begun to drink too much. Or you may have a game plan based on segregating the different parts of your life, something along the lines of 'I try not to take the office home with me.' If you have your own stress programme, conscious or unconscious, it is good to recognise it for what it is, so that you can decide if it is as effective as it could be. If you don't have a mechanism for defusing the pressure, and you do live with stress at work, it is worth thinking, now, about whether some of the ideas in this chapter could help you take more control over this aspect of your life.

One of the most interesting recent findings about work-related stress is that it is not the high-powered top guns and captains of industry who face the worst of it. It is the people who feel powerless and have little control over aspects of their working life who suffer the really deadly stress. And it is, literally, deadly. A massive 30,000-person, 20-year-long study of heart attack risk among British civil servants has suggested that feeling you have little control at work isn't just uncomfortable – it can kill you.

The study showed that levels of the key blood-clotting agent, fibrinogen, were directly related to the amount of control and autonomy each individual felt he or she had at work. Fibrinogen levels determine your likelihood of having a heart attack and are raised substantially by smoking and drinking. But having the feeling that you cannot control things around you at work was shown to raise fibrinogen readings almost as much as being a regular smoker. As a result, Whitehall mandarins, dealing with the pressures of vital government business and rewarded with pay and pensions reflecting these responsibilities, are not killed off by heart attacks at anything like the rate that affects the humble clerks and messengers, busy doing what they're told at the bottom of the civil service hierarchy.

The civil service research emphasises the importance of taking the initiative to manage the stress factors in your own situation. The starting point must be a careful look at where you feel helpless and powerless to affect your situation and circumstances. What, realistically, could you do to increase your control in these areas? You may find that you can have more autonomy and responsibility just by asking for it, especially if this has never been recognised as an issue before. Your line manager may appreciate your work and not mind at all, once the question is raised, where, when or in what order you do it. Alternatively, you may have to proceed by short stages and small victories, or actually subvert a rigid system in order to make space for yourself, as happens, inevitably, in every jail in the land. Your work should not be like a prison – and if it is, you should probably be making plans for your escape. But many organisations do slot people into restrictive, over-defined roles and procedures. If this has happened to you, it is up to you to make change happen, for your own good, though it is also likely to benefit your employer as well.

➡ LITTLE WINS MEAN A LOT

Middle managers with responsibility for running departments or work units can be just as hemmed in and balked, though usually in subtler ways, as the civil service clerks. Frustration is in the eye of the beholder. But being given impossible targets to hit, with tight budgets, inflexible procedural rules and not enough staff, can produce exactly the same sense of thwarted helplessness. This is where you may need to draw on the experience of colleagues in your organisation, who may have faced the same problems and found their own ways of creating a life-saving modicum of room to manoeuvre. Rub shoulders with those who seem to have made the system work for them. Spend time with them and learn what you can to introduce a little more flexibility into your own situation. If you can't make big changes and win big victories, get some small ones under your belt.

The technique of feeding on small victories is a key element in learning to manage your own performance more effectively by managing the state you are in at particular times. This can be a highly rewarding process, but it must begin from a basis of realism about where you start from. What do you find energising? What do you find debilitating and energy-sapping? What parts of your life do you tend to put on hold and not address until you absolutely have to?

> Make a written list, now, of the ten things you would like to have completed, at work or at home, that are never quite important enough to elbow their way to the top of your priorities. These tasks can haunt you like ghosts, yet most of them will take less time than you think when you finally get round to doing them. For each one you can knock off the list, you will feel a disproportionate upsurge of energy and a sense of achievement, satisfaction and psychic relief. So write the list and then pick them off one at a time. Even one task a week will be absurdly liberating, because of the payoff that's derived from feeling an increasing sense of control.

The essence of this is the kick we enjoy from getting closure, from wrapping up a task, wiping it off our list and erasing it from our consciousness. Suddenly we have reduced the cognitive strain of life. The budget spreadsheet has been finished, the government statistics return has been filed or the loft has been cleared out. There is one less thing to worry about, one item less to remember at some future time, and the relief is something to savour, even if the task was only ever a minor one. The same joy at being able to cross off one commitment surfaces whenever you hear a colleague utter the four sweetest words in the English language: 'Leave it to me.' This, of course, works in reverse as well. Finding the opportunity to tell your manager 'It'll be OK – leave it to me' is one of the best career moves you can make.

When you triumphantly swat small tasks off your own list, you give yourself a reminder that you can succeed. It is a matter of positive feedback loops again. Receiving ongoing behavioural proof of your capacity to succeed affects your beliefs about what is possible for you – and the brain scoops up the message without caring a jot about the fact that you have consciously engineered this heartening sequence of small victories. But it need not stop there. This technique of manufacturing positive reference experiences can be deliberately developed on a larger scale to help shape and expand your beliefs about what you are capable of achieving. Instead of waiting until you have had the fortifying experience of facing and overcoming spontaneously occurring challenges to build up your self-confidence, you can go looking for them. It is worth taking a moment to think, quite cold-bloodedly, 'What sort of experiences would help me to believe, realistically, that I was capable of going on to the next stage in my professional development?' You can then, at the very least, start keeping an eye open for instances where experiences of this kind of situation might be gained. And if they don't arise unprompted, there may be things you can do to help them along.

➡ HOW TO USE THE OUTCOME FRAME

As soon as you begin taking this kind of active hand in managing your resources, you will see countless opportunities to make small, positive interventions in the situations that are developing around you. You will be starting to manage the state you are in and recognising that this is not something that is beyond your power to influence. For example, it is often possible to make yourself more resourceful in relation to a business situation, simply by making a conscious choice about how you approach it. People, and organisations, are frequently very problem-oriented. They proceed by asking 'What's the problem?' and then trying to solve it. This betrays a mindset that may not always be the most useful one that is available.

If you start considering not 'What's wrong?' but 'What is it I really want?', you create a different way of thinking that is likely to lead to a different set of answers. Both ways are potentially useful, but the addition of the second introduces more options and more flexibility. The first question frames the situation as a problem; the second looks towards an outcome. The distinction might seem like an insignificant quibble over semantics, but it makes a real difference to the sort of answers that people come up with. This question of how an issue is framed has been explored and developed very thoroughly in NLP. The metaphor of choosing a frame when you picture a business situation and changing the frame when you wish to see it in a different light is a simple, strong and helpful device and offers a brisk way to break through the limitations of problem-centred thinking.

> To illustrate its surprising potential, it would be useful if you would take pen and paper and note down, now, a 'live' issue, personal or professional, that matters to you. Then, bearing the same issue firmly in mind, apply these two sets of questions to it and notice the differing responses that the questions trigger:

Problem frame	Outcome frame
What is my problem?	What do I want?
How long have I had it?	How will I know when I've got it?
Where does the fault lie?	What else will improve when I get it?
Who is to blame?	What resources do I have already that can help?
What is my worst experience with this?	What is something similar that I have succeeded in?
Why haven't I solved it yet?	What is the next step?

The problem frame questions may clarify the situation, but they also tend to point you towards the past, towards what has already happened. Though they can sometimes be useful in clarifying what has happened, people frequently report feeling demotivated or depressed when thinking things through in this way. It may be good for clarity, but it is not good for energising yourself. The contrast, when you use the outcome frame questions in the right-hand column, can be quite sharp. For most people, approaching the situation in this way feels more stimulating and more likely to provoke an imaginative, constructive response.

People who use this technique for the first time, simply reading off the questions and applying them to the issue at hand, are usually surprised to discover how much difference it can make. They say things such as 'I hadn't realised that some of these alternatives were possible', and often find that they are suddenly confident about what steps they should take next. There is no magic about this. It is just that each of the questions automatically steers you towards the future and the possibility of choosing between a number of courses of action – and how you decide to frame your experience and the issues facing you fundamentally affects your responses. A lot of the art of personal resource management is a matter of picking the right frame to help you get to grips with a situation. If you can train yourself to do this – and to know when to jolt yourself into a fresh perspective by radically changing the frame – you will be able to tap into much more of your own potential for ingenious and creative management.

We are buffeted by all sorts of outside pressures, some benign, but many arbitrary, self-serving, malicious, commercial or nihilistic. We can choose to take our hands off the tiller and let these external influences blow us where they will or we can take steps to retain a measure of control of our moods, the state we're in and the ways we look at the world. Since drift is debilitating and there's nothing to be gained by being pushed around by a random mixture of outside forces, there is a strong argument for managing those aspects of our motivation which are under our control. And the way we think is definitely something we can have some control over.

Example

Linford Christie ran 100 metres in 9.87 seconds in 1993 to set a

British record only a couple of hundredths slower than the world record. He firmly believed that the positive visualisation and motivation techniques he had refined for himself were an essential part of his armoury, enabling him to draw out more of the explosive athletic power within his body. But he was realistic enough to know that he could never release his full physical potential. There is always more to go for, as Einstein pointed out when he claimed that man uses just one-tenth of his brainpower.

➡ THE NINE-YEAR-OLD STRATEGIST

Some people develop strategies for easing themselves through life at a very early age. Observe a bright nine-year-old pacing himself by watching the mileometer on a 100-mile car journey. At the 20-mile mark, it's 'Only five miles and we'll be a quarter of the way'. At 25 miles, it's 'Have you noticed it's only about eight more miles till we're a third of the way there?' Then the long haul of nearly 17 miles to the next major landmark. But it's such a watershed that it's worth waiting for: 'Hurray, we're over half way, and in 16 miles we'll be two-thirds of the way there.' After that, there's the quick fix, less than nine miles further on, of passing the three-quarters mark and then you're cruising down the home straight.

The use of interim milestone points to stoke up the enthusiasm through the 25-33-50-66-75 sequence, giving five points of focus in the middle half of the journey, is actually very sophisticated. This boy is building in positive feedback loops, as recommended earlier, to pace himself, sustain his interest and give himself rewarding experiences as he goes along. He is creating a frame by imposing a shape on a journey that would otherwise seem like an amorphous and interminable lump of travelling. He is not doing it consciously, but that is no reason why we should not copy his methods when we see how well they serve him. Pragmatism is all. Whatever works, works.

The key to getting the most out of all the ideas and techniques mentioned in this chapter is to learn them, adapt and adopt them and integrate them into the way you manage yourself. This will bring you immediate benefits in terms of improved performance – more energy, less stress, more stamina and more resourcefulness –

which are bound to be noticed, eventually, by those you work with and manage. If the people around you begin to be curious about what is going on, it will give you the opportunity to enjoy the most instructive learning experience of all, by starting to teach others. This is always interesting and may be challenging, for there is a lot of well-honed cynicism in business circles. But even the most jaundiced commentator tends to be lost for words when the evidence builds up that your new ideas are helping you to achieve better results. In passing on these techniques and approaches, you will be enlarging your understanding of them and demonstrating your readiness to take the next step in the development of your own career, from manager to leader.

In a Nutshell   Resource Management

- **Marshal your own time and talents:**
  - Many people spend parts of the day in unresourceful states, working at less than full capacity.

- **There's an energy crisis in most people's lives:**
  - Most of us know we don't get enough sleep.
  - In energy terms, the linkage is more direct than people realise between brain and body.
  - The brain is roughly 3 lb of squishy meat, burning energy ten times as fast as other body tissue.

- **Get up and do something:**
  - Exercise gives increased oxygenation of the blood, greater stamina and better concentration.
  - It's empowering to feel you're actively in control of this part of your life.
  - We can become habituated to levels of stress and the baseline keeps being ratcheted up.
  - Do you need to drink 'just to unwind'?
  - The rising tide of stress can get to you before you realise it's there.

- **How do you handle your stress?**

  - What does your personal stress management programme involve?

  - The really deadly stress hits people who feel powerless and have little control in their work.

- **What could you do to increase your control?**

  - Perhaps just ask, especially if this hasn't been an issue before.

  - Work shouldn't be a prison – if it is, you should be planning your escape.

- **Little wins mean a lot:**

  - If you can't win big victories, get some small ones under your belt.

  - What do you find energising? What do you find debilitating and energy-sapping?

  - List ten things you would like to have completed.

  - Pick them off one at a time, even just one a week.

  - It feels good to get closure, wrapping up a task and wiping it from your consciousness.

  - Make allies by saying 'Leave it to me'.

  - When you swat small tasks, you remind yourself that you can succeed. Positive feedback loops again.

  - Ask yourself: 'What sort of experiences would help me to believe I was capable of going on to the next stage in my professional development?'

- **How to use the outcome frame:**

  - This is starting to manage the state you're in.

  - Consider not 'What's wrong?', but 'What is it I really want?' It creates a different way of thinking.

  - Switching from problem frame to outcome frame questions captures the initiative.

- Outcome frame thinking is much more likely to trigger a constructive response.
- Each outcome question steers you towards the future and towards choices.
- How you frame experience determines your response.
- Linford Christie believed his positive visualisation and motivation techniques were worth yards.

- **The nine-year-old strategist:**
  - Build in positive feedback loops.
  - Create a frame by imposing a shape on your 'journey'.
  - If people around you get curious, learn more by starting to teach others.
  - This is the next step in your career, from manager to leader.

Chapter 9
Remote Management

'The best effect of fine persons is felt after we have left their presence.'

(Ralph Waldo Emerson, 1839)

➡ HOW TO RETAIN CONTROL BEYOND TIME AND DISTANCE

The art of remote management is simple: the best managers are always there, even when they're not. You can probably think of people who are far away in terms of distance or time, yet who somehow seem to be here, connected and present in your life. They could be teachers, schoolfriends, early and influential managers or friends and relatives who now live in distant lands. They could even have been dead for many years. But we still feel a connection with them that counts for something. By contrast, most people can also think of others who may be all too insistently present, in purely factual terms, yet seem quite remote and irrelevant to our thinking and our behaviour. Remoteness, it is clear, is not just a matter of distance or time.

Remote management is a key business skill and one that is growing in importance all the time. In business, coercion never was a very effective long-term strategy and it is becoming more and more unacceptable now, just as today's fragmented, flexible and dispersed workforces are making it more and more unworkable. That leaves leadership and persuasion as the main tools available to managers. Where the New Manager scores over the old-style boss is in having the knack of drawing excellent performance out of teams and individuals, without having to be looking over shoulders all the time. If people work in certain ways because they are afraid, or because they are obeying rigid, prescriptive rules, or for the pleasure of doing down rivals, or because their pay is directly dependent on how much they complete, they are always in danger of being stumped by the first unusual, unconventional turn of events they encounter. If a person can operate with reasonable autonomy, with authority and responsibility delegated from his or her manager and a fairly clear sense of how that manager would respond to the situation, everything is different. Even improvised solutions to unprecedented problems will show the stamp of the absent manager's style and outlook, coupled with the flexible ingenuity that surfaces when people are given the chance to do the best they can. To understand how this ideal state of affairs can be created, it is worth looking in detail at how the general principles of the New Manager's approach apply to the special requirements of remote management.

First, lets be clear – we are all remote managers. If you have responsibility for a single team in an office 200 miles away or a network of branches in eight European capitals, using six different languages, it is obvious. If you manage a field maintenance operation, with dozens of engineers out on the road, or a small team of people who work in the office next door and whom you see every day, it may not be so apparent. Yet while your engineers are serving the customers, you might as well be an ocean or two away, for all the direct influence you can have on their performance. And the moment you absent yourself, either by going away on a business trip or a holiday or even just stepping into a meeting in the same building, your team members are working unsupervised, under nothing more than your remote control.

It would be extraordinary – and quite insulting – if your presence or absence had no effect at all on the behaviour of those you manage. But have you specifically thought about how your people function in your absence? Do they co-operate democratically, or does someone automatically assume control? If so, is everyone happy to work like this? And is the *de facto* leader the right person to be taking decisions? Some control freaks would like to believe everything goes on unchanged, whether they are there are not. They appoint deputies to work within strict guidelines and tight external controls and feel comforted by the rigidity of a framework that leaves little room for mistakes to occur. The bad news for this approach is, however, that mistakes will occur anyway. They don't need room or time or reasons. And when something does go wrong, a rigid, four-square structure is not the best for encouraging people to come up with off-the-cuff ideas about how to rectify the situation.

➡ DEVELOP PEOPLE'S COMPETENCE AND CONFIDENCE

Ultimately, you can't manage people at a distance without trusting them to think for themselves. Good managing is like good parenting, in that both are concerned with providing what's necessary to enable the individual to grow in both competence and confidence. The aim is to encourage increasing self-reliance, by judiciously intervening and refraining from intervening so that there is enough of a stretch to help the person learn, until eventually he or she is ready to operate independently. At the same time, it is vital that the demands that are made are not so great that the person is overwhelmed and demoralised. The parent who takes the time to show the children how to bake a cake is acting as a coach and mentor, as well as delivering pure instruction. The child's first cake may not be perfect and it may take three times as long as usual to make. But the investment of time, patience and attention now may pay off in decades of home-made cakes in the future. It may also have a benign effect on the children's confidence, on gender stereotyping and on their appreciation of the care and commitment shown by the flour-spattered parent. One of the dangers inherent in the bustle of a busy family life, or an overstretched office, is that parents and managers lose sight of the fact that the development of their juniors must be seen as an important objective. It is all too easy for the person who has handled the job a hundred times before to nudge people aside and say: 'Never mind – I'll do it.' If this happens frequently at work, the lack of delegation and task-specific training is unstimulating for individuals who may be keen to learn new skills. It also condemns the manager to continue taking the controls every time a similar situation occurs in future.

As the people you manage grow in competence and confidence, under your guidance, both their usefulness to your company and their potential employability elsewhere (including in the offices of your competitors) are enhanced. This is desirable for them – and obviously desirable for your company, up to the point where offers of more money and responsibility or dissatisfaction with policy or personalities cause them to want to move on. The better you train them and the further they can see themselves progressing, the longer you will keep them and the more productive they will be.

Ask yourself: 'What does this person need – now and in the future – so that he or she can achieve more?' If you can put yourself in someone else's shoes long enough to recognise the right answers, you will be able to create a working environment that leads and stimulates, rather than cramping and confining people. In that sort of context, remote management becomes more like coaching than controlling and it makes far less difference, on a day-to-day basis, whether you are on the spot, on a plane or out on the road.

➡ MAKING YOUR MARK

If you have close contact, at least part of the time, and some sort of personal relationship with those you are responsible for, remote management is largely an extension of what you would be doing anyway. But there are cases where you are starting from scratch and even the word 'remote' seems like an understatement. These can give us valuable insights that have some general applications. What follows here is based on executive coaching Ian McDermott has done with several clients who found themselves in exactly this position.

Imagine you have just been appointed to a new post with the title of Business Development Manager, Northern Europe. This is obviously an exciting and challenging opportunity, but you are going to need a clear strategy and a great deal of energy to ensure that you get off to a good start. Suddenly, you are responsible for markets you know nothing about, run by people you don't know, who do not have English as their first language, and to whom you are a complete unknown. What can you do immediately to begin to get to grips with the situation and minimise the remoteness that's built into it? There are three steps that need to be taken:

• Find out about the people and companies involved.

• Establish a presence.

• Make your vision clear and show your people the way forward.

The way you go about finding out about the people and organisations will give your new people plenty of information about you and your approach. Geographically remote management calls for subtle and sophisticated use of signs and gestures and one of the first signals you need to send is that you intend to be a leader, rather than a caretaker. Ask your market managers and product group managers to think about how they want to position themselves and how they would prioritise the issues that affect their areas. The approach should be something like this:

'I'm new and I need to know what's important to you. What are your achievements? What are our strengths, as a group, in your market? What are the key areas where more investment or improved performance could offer us significant returns?'

You can ask these questions in an introductory letter, which presupposes that replies will come back to you in written form, or in group meetings. But whatever method you choose, this opening gambit needs to be followed up, as soon as possible, with individual, face-to-face meetings.

Establishing a presence begins with giving your new team the chance to put a face to your name. If there is no alternative, you may have to call the key people in to see you on your home ground. But it is very much better if you can put in the time and effort to visit each of them on site. You can pick up so much detailed information just by keeping your eyes and ears open, watching how people relate to each other and comparing what you are told with the evidence of your senses. Remember, too, that the person you have come to see cannot help being more relaxed and revealing more of himself or herself in familiar, comfortable surroundings. You will always get to know people's strengths and weaknesses more quickly if you can observe them in their native habitats. But the purpose of these trips is not just scouting or information-gathering. They are also your opportunity to introduce yourself and make a clear statement about what kind of manager you are.

As far as the people you have assumed responsibility for are concerned, you are a new product. They know little about you and have yet to be convinced that your appointment is necessarily a godsend. Careful product positioning, with yourself as the product, will enable you to influence perceptions of you and your management style and ensure that neither your own boss nor your new team will misunderstand what you are about. If this sounds a little cold-blooded and mechanical, don't forget that nature abhors a vacuum. If you don't project a positive and purposeful image, some less useful image will surface to fill the gap. So make it clear who you are and what your approach is going to be. Make it clear that you are not an exclusively procedural manager, bent on laying down a Napoleonic Code of rules and regulations and then expecting to enjoy a quiet life while everyone goes through the motions without rocking the boat. At the other extreme, you must avoid giving the impression of purveying windy rhetoric, without the attention to detail that makes sure things get done. The inspirational manager who talks a good game and fires people up without ensuring that the necessary competence and resources are in place to complete the task is a danger to shipping and a particular peril to those who work under him or her. People know this and are understandably wary, so they will be waiting for the reassurance of seeing you signal a balanced attention to both means and ends.

Making the vision clear is the third part of the remote manager's short-term action plan. This means showing people that there is a way forward and that you and they can both be clear about where the company is going and what it is trying to achieve. This helps to place each part of your team's daily activity in a larger context that makes sense of it and gives it purpose. It can also take personal issues, such as resentment of your appointment in place of a popular predecessor, out of the immediate firing line, allowing everyone to be aligned and focused together on the journey ahead.

➡ A CRAVING FOR CONNECTEDNESS

The hallmark of success in remote management is the ability to take the remoteness out of it. All the familiar late-twentieth-century clichés about being alone in a crowd or lonely in the city can apply to groups of people just as much as to individuals. A whole branch office of 50 or 100 people can feel just as isolated as a shipping agent working on his own in some foreign port or a sales rep who doesn't see her base from one week to the next. It is the manager's job to integrate people and groups into a team or community, whatever the distances involved. People need to feel connected and there are many new technologies, from video-conferencing to the World Wide Web, that can help to make it possible. The Internet fanatics who spend hours on-line do so not because they are information junkies, as is often suggested, but because they are connection junkies, revelling in the feeling of being connected and part of something that feels big, inclusive and significant and that spans the globe on a 24/7 basis. If you assume it's the information that matters, then a sheaf of hard copy from an exchange of views on the Net would mean just as much as the real-time dialogue itself. But it isn't the information, it's the connection – and the feeling of membership of something that transcends all the normal limitations of mundane factors like time, geography and cost. But if connectedness is what your people need, how does the remote manager satisfy that need?

The first priority is to build physical and organisational connections. As recently as the mid 1980s, the options for communication with your people would have been restricted to telephoning, using the telex, sending telegrams or writing letters. Now we have lost the telex, but gained faxes, e-mails, mobile phones, text pagers, video-conferencing, voicemail, intranets, the Internet and the World Wide Web. This extraordinary explosion of technologies, coupled with rapid falls in the real cost of telecom services, has shrunk the world and made it possible for international teams to work together in completely new ways. But setting up appropriate communications links needs to be matched by a similar commitment to setting up suitable channels for two-way flows of information. People in remote locations need to be able to get in touch with the right people in your department to ask advice, to report on progress, or to let you know the background to what is happening in their markets. The Harvard Business School slogan 'Think global, act local' only makes sense if the global thinking is informed by feedback coming in from the world outside.

Having set up the connections, the next task is to make the people you are managing *feel* connected, which is not necessarily the same thing. To be able to foster a sense of belonging to a company or a division, to your team, to a group with a set of shared goals, is a sign of great skill and finesse in a manager, especially if the people involved are scattered far and wide. One way to do it is to actively encourage communication that goes beyond the purely functional. Another important factor is making sure that those in remote locations have direct access to the resources they need, so that they know who they can contact for specific technical help or more generalised advice based on past experience. It is important, for example, that every office always has up-to-date copies of the latest internal telephone directory or extension numbers list. The more intricate the web of cross-connections, the greater the number of different people who are co-operating with each other and exchanging views and information, the more connected the various parts of the organisation will feel.

➡ MAKE PEOPLE WANT TO BE PART OF YOUR TEAM

The most crucial part of this whole issue of connectedness is making your people, wherever they are, feel that they are connected to you and that they want to be associated with your team. There is no mystery about how this can be achieved – just regard your staff as your customers. You need to give them certain things that they want, if you are to inspire their confidence, commitment and loyalty. Ask yourself three questions:

- 'What is it about me and my management style, specifically, that would make people want to feel they were part of my team?'
- 'How can I serve their interests and raise their standing in the company?'

- 'What can I do that my people can identify with with pleasure or pride?'

Do you champion your people and their ideas? Do you build positive visibility within the organisation for yourself and your team? Do you achieve success and ensure that your people share the credit for it? If people feel good about working for you, they will set their own standards and targets at far more ambitious levels than you would ever try to impose. They will still feel connected, however seldom they actually find themselves in the same room as you, and they will want to spend time with you, try out ideas on you, ask for support and advice and tell you what they have been doing, whenever they have a chance to do so. For your part, you should create opportunities for this sort of contact by turning up in person whenever you can, talking to people, phoning them, faxing them newspaper cuttings ('I wonder if you saw this in Saturday's *FT*? What do you make of it?') and generally signalling that both teams and individuals, near and far, are always in your thoughts. It pays real dividends if you can find ways to make your people feel valued. It is even more powerful if you can make them feel special.

Example

In one of Britain's largest and most efficient customer care call centres, the phones are ringing every hour of the day and night. Several companies use the call centre's services, but the staff are in no doubt about which of these clients they feel is the most prestigious to work with. Everyone in the building is doing a generically similar job, dealing with similarly anguished or disgruntled customers. Yet the people at the call centre compete vigorously for the honour of joining the dedicated group that services the top client. Within the area where this elite team works, there are special carpets with the client company's logo and people wear branded uniform jackets. The staff are still employed by the call centre, but there is no mistaking the pride and brand loyalty these people feel towards their client, an upmarket European car company. Every one of them has driven the client's cars. Every one of them has been away on specific team training courses in luxurious and stimulating settings. Care has been taken to give individuals the authority to carry each job through to a satisfactory resolution of the customer's problem, with great emphasis laid on the commercial value of the word-of-mouth publicity that comes from such successes – 'the campaign money can't buy'. There has been a genuine investment in making the people feel special and the result is high levels of job satisfaction and astonishing levels of performance. The fact that the client company's top management is geographically located a couple of countries away does not make a scrap of difference. These people are about as connected as it's possible to be.

➡ DIRECTION, FAITH AND ENERGY

As a general management strategy, there is no doubt that making your people feel special is a sound approach. If their levels of skill and intellectual attainment are not obviously awe-inspiring, it is part of the manager's function to set goals and put in place the motivation to achieve some worthwhile targets. A newly fired ambition to chalk up record-breaking productivity improvements (even from a low base), to deliver superb customer service or to develop ideas for a much enhanced product can bring job satisfaction into situations where people have become used to simply turning up, doing their time and taking the money. It is probably an exaggeration to say there are no bad workforces, only bad managers. But good managers can and do work wonders, simply by giving clear direction, demonstrating faith in their people and conveying their own energy and enthusiasm. There is no escape for the manager who fails in his duty to his or her people. Whatever happens, you will be identified with those you manage, whether you like it or not.

Example

The most dispiriting workplace we have ever visited was a large, modern and apparently profitable print works in South London, managed, remotely, by a small coterie of executives in a neat little office on the edge of the City. These managers talked cheerfully of expansion and takeovers. The print shop manager was less sanguine. Asked 'What are your staff like?', he replied sourly: 'Baboons – only not so trustworthy.' The top managers went ahead with refining plans for a Stock Exchange listing. The people who had been labelled baboons lived up to the expectations of them. The print manager, who had always been regarded by management as something of a zoo-keeper, said 'I told you so', and blamed the fact that the directors were never seen around the factory and had no idea what was going on. The quality of work went downhill, customers deserted in droves and the company spiralled down into bankruptcy at a rate that shook even those familiar with the traditional volatility of the printing industry. Management remoteness and the failure to make front-line staff feel wanted, needed or in any way special had pitchforked the company into oblivion in a matter of months.

➡ HOW CAN I MAKE MY PEOPLE STAND OUT AS SPECIAL?

If you ask yourself the question 'How are my people and their functions special?', you should be able to come up with some positive aspects. If you don't know, why should they? And if they are really not special, you are going to have to start thinking quickly about how they might become so. How would the organisation, its products or the service it offers suffer if your group's activity stopped dead for ever at five o'clock this afternoon? Would everything grind to a halt? You are looking for added value, here, and the most graphic way to identify it is often by examining the subtracted value that would be felt if your people were not there and doing a good job. Do others, outside your department, realise how crucial your team's role is? And if they don't, what are you going to do now to raise its profile and ensure that its importance is recognised? Recognition is vital for morale, as well as being the principal defence against cost-cutting redundancy programmes.

At the same time, every improvement you can cultivate in the skills base and know-how of your people will affect not just the perception but the substance. It is good that they should be recognised as skilled and special. It is even better if they are genuinely developing new talents and capabilities to make them even more special. But this is not just a matter of learning more formal skills, like how to use the latest version of PowerPoint or an accounting software package. It is also to do with developing the skills of self-management, so that your people can operate successfully and confidently at a distance from you, with only light touches on the tiller. The further away they are, the more you are bound to rely on them to be self-organising and the more important it is to have in place good feedback loops to ensure that reliable information is streamed back to you.

➡ THE SELF-ORGANISING TEAM

Teaching people to be self-organising is the subject for another book all to itself. It is a complex business, but we suggest concentrating on eight key qualities that you will need to foster in the people you must lead and motivate from afar. Your aim should be to teach them to:

- be proactive
- take ownership of issues
- be prepared to make mistakes
- learn from mistakes
- follow through to completion
- recognise achievement (their own and other people's)
- take credit for success
- install workable feedback systems.

If you can appoint or develop people with the right technical and industry expertise for the job, coupled with this range of basic self-management skills, you will be able to delegate with confidence, whether you are concerned with leaving the office for a few days or remotely managing an outpost of your organisation on the other side of the globe.

In a Nutshell **Remote Management**

- **Retain control beyond time and distance:**
  - We are all remote managers; even being in a meeting means your team is unsupervised.

- **Develop people's competence and confidence:**
  - What does this person need so that he or she can achieve more?

- **Making your mark:**
  - Find out about the people and companies involved.
  - Establish a presence.
  - Make your vision clear and show the way forward.
  - Give the new team the chance to put a face to your name.
  - Make a clear statement about what kind of manager you are.
  - Signal balanced attention to both means and ends.

- **The craving for connectedness:**
  - Build physical and organisational connections.
  - Encourage communication beyond the purely functional.
  - Make sure people in remote locations have direct access to resources.

- **Make people want to be part of your team:**
  - What is it that would make people want to feel part of your team?
  - How can you serve their interests and raise their standing in the company?
  - What can you do that your people can identify with?

- **Champion your people and their ideas:**
  - Give direction, faith and energy.

- **How can you make your people stand out as special?**
  - Look for added value.
  - Create the self-organising team.

Chapter 10
Leading, Chunking and Delegating

'A pile of rocks stops being a pile of rocks the moment one person looks at it, carrying in his mind the vision of a cathedral.'

(Antoine de Saint-Exupery, 1942)

➡ FROM MANAGING TO LEADING: HOW TO INCREASE YOUR INFLUENCE

Leadership is one of those words that has too many negative associations for some people, yet leading, rather than bossing, is what every modern manager is supposed to be learning to do. There is a general recognition that the ability to manage people's performance by encouraging, supporting, inspiring, guiding, coaxing, coaching, correcting, developing and leading by example is a rare and precious talent – and one that brings benefits for both the organisation and the people who are led.

The New Manager needs to be a leader. But where do the qualities a leader needs come from? There is only one possible answer: from inside yourself. Luckily, however, you have already shown unmistakable evidence of your ability to function successfully as a leader.

Leadership as an abstraction is a virtually meaningless idea. It is only achieved by doing, by the act of leading. And we have all done it in a variety of different contexts – as a parent, as an older brother or sister, in a playground gang or a Sunday school group, or as the person with the knowledge of how to put up wallpaper or strip down an engine or make curtains or swim or ride a horse and who shows someone else how it is done. We have all done plenty of following, but we have all taken the lead as well. We know what leadership feels like, from the inside. We are leaders, when the circumstances are right. So the question is not 'Will I be a leader?', it is 'How do I lead?', swiftly followed by 'How do I want to lead?'

Like charity, leadership begins at home. If you aspire to be a convincing and successful leader in the work context, by leading others, it is important to look at how you lead yourself. How do you score against that list of leadership activities – encouraging, supporting, inspiring, guiding, coaxing, coaching, correcting, developing and leading by example – in relation to the way you handle yourself? Do you give yourself real credit for your strengths, recognise and take pleasure from your successes and treat yourself with generosity when the results you achieve are less than perfect? When a mistake occurs, despite your best efforts, do you make sure all the useful learning is derived from it and then forgive yourself easily and put the incident behind you, so that it does not get the chance to cast a long emotional shadow? If the way you manage your own resources, talents and emotions is flexible and magnanimous, this approach will readily transfer across to become the basis for successful management and leadership. If it isn't, how do you think this is affecting the way you lead others?

➡ YOU'RE A LEADER, BUT HOW DO YOU DO IT?

Just as everyone has had experience of leading, everyone has an individual leadership style. It is worth asking yourself what your leadership style is like. What comes naturally to you? What do you actually do when you are in a leadership role? Bearing in mind that leadership is largely about influencing people, how do you endeavour to influence others? Being a leader demands that you have a vision, however modest, of something more than has currently been achieved or realised and that you can influence people so that it engages their hearts and minds. But leadership presupposes something about the scale of the enterprise, too – that it should be something beyond the merely trivial. Someone can influence you to have another drink or to join them in tucking into the tiramisu at the end of your business lunch, but that hardly qualifies. Leadership leads somewhere. Perhaps the best practical definition would be that it is 'influence in the service of something greater than the specific action or activity that is to hand'.

Your personal leadership style is about how you enlist the co-operation of others. Whether it will be accepted and successful or not will depend partly on whether those others see your approach as leading or manipulating. The touchstone for this is their sense of whether they are being exploited or not. They will not object to your success, nor to your enjoying the fruits of it, if they are getting something out of the deal, too. People have an exquisitely subtle feeling for these matters. They want to feel that what benefits you also brings them benefits, in terms of cash or kudos, satisfaction or job security, power or prominence, or any one of a dozen other payoffs. There are no rules, but influential leaders are careful to maintain some visible linkage between the effort and commitment their people put in and the rewards that come to them.

Besides demonstrating to your people that you are all pulling in the same direction, you will also need to communicate with them on many different levels, if you are to be a successful leader. You may have a unique vision of the future, embracing ambitious and complicated long-term goals, but you will also need to find efficient ways of communicating what needs to be done on Monday morning. One of the core skills for the New Manager is developing the ability to recognise how individual people feel most comfortable receiving information and learning how to match their needs. This is vital, because of the requirement to inform and influence the people you report to, and possibly customers and suppliers, as well as those you manage. Don't assume senior managers will all be big-picture, helicopter-vision strategists, nor that people lower down the business hierarchy will slot neatly into a pyramid diagram that calls for earnest, plodding, unambitious, fine-detail-obsessed worker ants.

➡ **THE OVERVIEW AND THE DETAIL**

People at all different levels like to handle information in different chunk sizes – and the extremes can be spectacular. You just have to ask a mundane question such as 'What have you been doing today?' to unleash live demonstrations of vastly different preferences. Some answers will be terse summaries, a couple of headlines built around people or events and highlighting the most unusual or dramatic aspects of the working day. Other people will begin 'Well, I got up about seven, had a shower and was on the road by eight o'clock, so I got in here at 8.45, before the porter was even on duty at Reception ...' This kind of chronological precision is the trademark of a particular type of small-chunk, fine-detail operator. Dyed-in-the-wool specimens will even react to interruptions by rewinding to a convenient milestone and picking up the tale again in almost the same words ('Where was I? – Yes, so 8.45, and the porter wasn't even in yet, but I went up to the office and read my e-mail and ...'). In any team, you are likely to find both styles.

It is obvious that CEOs, MDs and chairmen, charged with planning the strategic future of their companies, must have at least some big-picture tendencies. But it does not follow that the small-chunker's attention to detail is not wanted in senior management, even at boardroom level. Engineering, the sciences and accountancy all demand this precise, cautious and analytical gene, so it is quite possible that a large company's production director, research director and finance director could all be more at home with detailed, fine-grained information than broad, sweeping visions.

Those who instinctively package information into pithy, concise bullet points when they are giving it out invariably like to receive information and briefings in the same crisp, condensed format. They quickly become impatient and irritated with small-chunkers and may well fail to pick up vital details that they need to know, which can have serious repercussions for negotiations, production or even safety. This kind of breakdown in communications is a daily occurrence in many offices and both parties are usually quite unable to see how they have contributed to the mess.

Example

'I couldn't stand there all day, listening to him wittering on,' says one side, briefly. 'If he had something important to say, why didn't he draw my attention to it?'

From the other perspective, of course, the same situation looks completely different. 'I was trying to warn him about things that were likely to cost the firm thousands of pounds, and all he could do was stand there, tapping his foot and looking over my shoulder at the people in the back office. I gave him all the facts and told him three times over that we needed a decision today, but he just didn't seem to be listening.' The complainant is right: by that stage, he wasn't.

Detail specialists need to take the trouble to edit their material to suit the needs of the people they are talking to. That means pushing the important content up to the front, thinning out the facts and figures to focus on one or two that are memorable or representative, speaking with conviction and emphasis, taking account of whether you are meeting for 30 seconds on the stairs or 30 minutes in an office and really working to point out the relevance of your news to the person you are talking to. There is a useful and universal NLP guideline that is relevant here, which states that 'the meaning of a communication is the response it triggers'. In other words, you are responsible for making sure people you talk to understand what you mean. If they don't get the message, it's not their fault. It's your responsibility, because you have yet to put it across in a form that is meaningful to them.

But it is not just unskilled or inconsiderate communication by the small-chunker that has caused the problem described above. The egocentric impatience of the big-chunk man has led him to glaze over and switch off, on the assumption that he will not be missing anything of importance. If he had had crucial facts to impart, he would have made his point strongly in the first few seconds, so he assumes everyone would have done the same. In his eyes, the fact that his colleague is still talking after a couple of minutes more or less proves he has nothing else to do with his time. To deal with other people as if they all had the same mindset, abilities and needs as himself demonstrates arrogance, inflexibility and a damaging lack of practical intelligence. After all, it's not simply a question of whether it is possible to stay focused during a long speech with too much tedious detail. That, too, depends on the way your mind approaches it. Many people may doze off in court while the judge drones his way through a complicated summing up, but the defendant is seldom one of them.

Individuals at opposite ends of the chunk size continuum can seem like life forms from different galaxies, with no common language and little tolerance for each other's pecularities. And of course the great mass of employees in any company or organisation will naturally fall somewhere between these two extremes, though everybody seems to have an instinctive bias, one way or the other. But every manager should remember that one of the characteristics of outstanding leaders is the ability to operate effectively at both levels, up with the big picture and down among the fine details, and to move easily between them as circumstances dictate.

➡ THE MAGIC OF CHUNKING

The whole business of information chunk size is so central to the way people act and communicate at work that every manager needs to understand its implications. Despite the phenomenal memory and associative capacity of the human brain, there is a fairly clear limit to the number of items of information we can handle and process at any one moment. There is a small amount of variation between individuals, but this limit, identified in a series of experiments by psychologist George A. Miller in the mid 1950s, is generally taken to be about 7 ± 2 bits of information – between five and nine. This can be seen in practice if you play a few simple games concerned with remembering number sequences. Can you, for example, recall the following eleven-number sequence after looking at it for a few seconds and then covering it up?

42714430104

Most people find this memory task difficult and mildly uncomfortable, even to attempt. It is certainly at or near the limits of what we can cope with. But if the digits are arbitrarily separated into smaller groups, the task of memorising the sequence starts to become significantly less daunting. Here is the same number string, chopped up into three groups:

427 144 30104

That was noticeably easier, wasn't it? And if the same figures are rearranged into something that, for British readers, is a familiar standardised format, like this,

0171 240 3444

it becomes very straightforward to recognise it as an inr er London telephone number, though you still wouldn't know, until you rang it, that it was the main switchboard number for Orion Publishing, the company responsible for the Business Toolkit series and hence for this book.

Any feeling of confusion and being overwhelmed that was engendered by the first inexorable string of 11 digits was considerably lessened by a change of chunk size, breaking the run of numbers down into two threes and a five, sequences which carried no apparent meaning but were at least short enough not to trigger the feeling of overload. When the further rearrangement of the figures gave meaning to the whole string and made it crystallise into a recognisable phone number format, any brain strain was vastly reduced. As long as you recognised 0171 as the inner London prefix, that four-digit group need now count as only one bit, leaving you with the task of remembering that one prefix plus seven additional digits – eight bits altogether – and bringing it within the 7 ± 2 range. All this, of course, explains why remembering overseas telephone numbers is often so difficult; they are the same digits, but they chunk them differently. If you are to encode information in your memory, learn it and call it back into consciousness when you need to, it is essential to chunk masses of raw data down into a size and format that works for you. You also need to know, in comparison with other people, what your own chunk-size bias is, so that you can make allowance for this in the ways you approach managing and being managed.

➡ STEPPING UP THE CHUNK SIZE

If you are most comfortable dealing with matters of detail and you tend to shy away from thinking in terms of big pictures and broad principles, there is a useful mental exercise you can do to practise and train yourself in this area. You need to shift your habits of thinking upwards from the small-chunk detail to the wider context, which means moving from the particular to the general. You learn to do this by thinking of an object – let's say, that little pile of A4 on your desk – and asking yourself 'What is this an example of?' With not a moment's hesitation, you reply: 'Paper.' Now go round again. What is paper an example of? Stationery, perhaps. And stationery is an example of? Office supplies. And office supplies are examples of? Purchases. And purchases exemplify? Traded goods. And traded goods are examples of? Products. And products are examples of? Things. Not hugely enlightening, you might think. But if your sales manager's answer to the question 'What's on that desk?' is an airy 'Oh, a few things' and your chief accountant's answer is 'Five sheets of white A4 paper, blank, probably about 70 gsm,' you have the aforementioned galaxies in miniature – and the mutually uncomprehending life forms, too.

Practising this technique of stepping up the chunk size and escalating from the specific to the general is particularly important if your own instincts tend towards the miniaturist. It is equally useful if you have an impeccably balanced world-view but want to find the verbal and conceptual vocabulary to manage others who tend to spiral off into the wide blue yonder and talk in relentlessly detail-free big-picture generalities. This is where the pacing and leading we talked about earlier must be brought into play. To get through to these people and encourage them to take more notice of the practicalities of life and the sometimes irksome details that have to be accounted for, you will need to begin by talking to them in the sort of language they understand. This is how you engage and hold people's attention, by taking them as you find them, meeting them on their home ground and then leading them towards the different perspective you want them to try out.

By training yourself to step upwards and think in big-chunk terms, you are broadening the range of techniques available to you in managing people. You will also find these exercises useful in jolting your own thinking out of a rut when you are trying to arrive at creative solutions to business challenges. People are always imploring you to look at problems from a fresh perspective; this is a simple technique to help you do it. The basic question 'What is this an example of?' can be augmented with 'What could this be a part of?' in contexts where it seems to fit more comfortably and the exercise should always be pressed a little farther than you think it will go. The staircase of answers can usually be pushed to five steps or more from almost any starting point. If you began with 'Chardonnay', for example, you might step up to 'white wine', 'wine', 'alcoholic beverage', 'drink' and 'liquid'.

➡ GO TO MEET SMALL-CHUNKERS AT THEIR LEVEL OF DETAIL

Getting in tune with big-picture people is one part of the manager's job. But it is equally important to be able to communicate with people whose focus is captured by matters of fine detail. As well as chunking upwards, you need to be able to chunk down. You can practise doing this in much the same way, with questions that provoke movement in the small-chunk direction, such as 'What would be an aspect of this?', 'What is a specific example of X?' and 'What is a part of this?' If you started with, say, 'profitability', this might lead you down the steps to 'new products', and then to the specific product being launched next month. Or you might go in a completely different direction – there is no one correct sequence.

Sometimes this can become more than an exercise. In a technology-driven organisation – in electronics, perhaps, or pharmaceuticals – a quick trot down the line of thinking that reminds key players how dependent your future is on the strength of your lab work might be a salutary reminder of the real priorities of your business. As with stepping up, try to practise stepping down at least five levels each time. When you identify people as definite small-chunkers, consciously go to meet them on the fine-grained detail level. Signal your concern for the things that are dear to their hearts by talking or asking about real figures, specifications, dates and technicalities. Show that you can and do think like them, before encouraging them to join you in looking at some of the bigger issues affecting the department, the company or the industry as a whole.

There are several clues that can help you spot a clear-cut big picture person or a dedicated small-chunker quickly enough to be useful to you at first meeting. Characteristic big-chunk lines are 'What does this boil down to?', or 'Just give us the headlines', or

'What would we achieve by doing that?', or even the classic 'Do me a memo on a compliments slip telling me why we should go ahead.' Small-chunkers say things like 'Can I see the detail on that later?', or 'What exactly are you expecting?', or 'How, precisely, are we going to get it done on time?', and are generally more likely to see objections to daring or grandiose plans than their big-chunk colleagues. Big picture people bring obvious strengths of vision, ambition and strategic awareness to the organisation, offset at times by a lack of clarity about the hurdles to be overcome and the practical resources needed to achieve implementation. Small-chunk people can save your ad campaign by picking up mistakes in copy. They can save your life by insisting on meticulous checking of heavy machinery, or save your lawsuit by dredging through the files for some crucial scrap of evidence. They can equally well drive you to distraction with their desire for extra decimal places and their frozen inability to take decisions on the basis of incomplete data. It is almost impossible to imagine a successful company that did not boast a mixture of the two types. Indeed, the recipe for success often seems to require the presence of one or two extremists from both camps, to balance out the moderation of the majority.

Even if you had never come across a discussion of people's chunk size proclivities before today, you must, by now, have a shrewd idea of our own inclinations. The stepping up and stepping down exercises described earlier should ideally be used, over a period of weeks, to assist in training yourself to operate easily and comfortably at both the big picture and small-chunk levels. Knowing this aspect of yourself is important, because it helps you remain alert to some of the possible drawbacks. For example, big picture people can sometimes fall down on operational implementation. And if you are very good at small chunk work, you may find it difficult to delegate. Small chunking and obsessive micromanagement of every aspect of the situation are familiar bedfellows.

➡ THE FIRST STEP IN DELEGATION IS SELF-DELEGATION

As management progresses towards leadership, the ability to assess tasks accurately and assign them to appropriate people, so that you can turn away and focus on other matters, is a priceless asset. You can make rapid progress in the art of delegation by examining how good you are at self-delegation. If you have a number of tasks to complete, do you try to do everything at once, or do you make a list of priorities and work your way down it, tackling one job at a time? If there is one overridingly important and difficult issue, do you try to take it head on? Or do you, as folk wisdom has always advised, make a point of giving yourself time to sleep on it? Many effective and experienced leaders have learned to trust the parts of their brains that operate out of sight, delegating the really tricky problems to the unconscious as part of a deliberate strategy. When they know a big decision is looming, especially if incomplete information means it cannot be a wholly rational, calculated choice, they will scan their briefing notes or other relevant material once and then get on with something else, apparently forgetting about the main issue. This is quite deliberate delegation, an invitation to the unpredictable and unbiddable powers of the brain to mull it over and see if they can come up with anything useful. The idea is to give the issue some incubation time, to allow the brain's unconscious creativity to come into play. They sleep on it, shower on it, drive down the motorway on it and hold it in the back of their minds for a day or two, without trying to push it to the forefront. As decision time approaches, they change gear into a fully focused, well briefed, conventionally rational mode of operation, but often discover, to their surprise, that they are bringing with them ideas about the problem that they didn't know they'd had.

The idea of delegating to ourselves is so unexpected that it is valuable to recognise just how much we can and do delegate all the time, to different parts of our brains. When the manager mentioned above was driving down the motorway, with his problem subconsciously simmering on the back burner, he was not consciously controlling his breathing, pulse rate and blood pressure, his sweat or insulin secretion levels or the digestion of his dinner. This was all under the control of his autonomic nervous system. He was not aware that he was humming along, quite loudly, to the *Ride of the Valkyries* on the tape deck. He was not even consciously aware of sending messages to his right foot and to both hands to signal, swing out and overtake the car in front. What he thought he was thinking about was stopping soon to buy some more petrol. With all this going on, though, there was still plenty of brain capacity left for other thoughts to come and go, for the manager to absorb and react to messages from roadside signs, for an itch on his knee to come to his attention and for immediate evasive action to be taken if something unexpected happened on the road ahead of him. Einstein's idea that we use one-tenth of our brains may be more of an image than a calculation, but it's a reminder that we have room inside for a limitless amount of activity, conscious and unconscious.

Just as self-delegation teaches you to trust in the possibility of good ideas coming out of the blue, delegating to others can be a remarkably heartening process. People can almost always do more than you, or they, think they can. And every project you brief someone else on automatically goes through the self-delegation process, because your brain is listening in on what you are saying. Your brain is working on it, too, behind the scenes, even though your desk is clear.

➡ LIVING WITH RISKS AND LEARNING FROM MISTAKES

The art of delegating successfully revolves around judging manageable risk. If you pass too much risk off on to a relatively inexperienced person, that is just irresponsibility. Too little risk and you might as well do it yourself – a situation which will continue, as you have just missed an opportunity to give your junior a significant piece of on-the-job training. Leaders have to trust their people to take reasonable risks, to back their judgements and to make errors from time to time. They have to show and train them to accept mistakes as feedback, rather than failure, and signal clearly that learning lessons is approved of, while covering tracks or shifting blame is not.

In fact, the manager's way of responding to mistakes is often the key factor in his or her team's success, since it impinges so directly on the self-esteem and confidence of each individual. Managers who behave as if their people's mistakes are wilful and deliberate are missing one of the major points about work and motivation, which is that human behaviour is, in the main, purposeful. Very few people come to work in the morning with the intention of doing a bad job and making themselves feel awful. Even the selfish, the embittered, the tetchy and those with a chip on their shoulder seldom go to work to fail. So when mistakes are made, don't assume that those who made them did it in order to lower their own self-esteem and be recognised as bad at their jobs. Instead, get curious.

The New Manager is aware of the many strands of motivation that combine to persuade people to get up and come to work, not least through taking a look inside to see what motives seem to be driving his or her own behaviour. Why do you go to work? You may say it is only to pay the mortgage, but would you really stop immediately and for ever if you won the lottery? What about factors such as meeting people, status, opportunities to prove your worth and win recognition, the feeling of doing something worthwhile and even building and reinforcing your sense of who you are?

> Spend a few minutes trying to list *everything* you get out of going to work. The more insight you can acquire into your own motives, the more understanding you will have of other people's.

As a leader, you need to recognise that what your people do is only a means to an end – or, more likely, to many different ends. It is when you know what an individual's motives are that you can start to lead effectively. If the person in question really did work only to pay her mortgage, you might well be able to lead her by offering new ways of paying it. Yet if you suggest switching to mugging, arms smuggling or high-pressure selling of holiday timeshares, you might find that considerations of ethics, personal safety and job satisfaction were revealed as other elements in the motivational package. If people come to work for a mixture of financial and other reasons, trying to lead and motivate them just by offering more money can actually be counterproductive. They'll take it – who wouldn't? – but they may still feel disappointed and demotivated that their other needs have not been recognised. If the missing factor is recognition and the sense of having done a good job, no amount of money will compensate for its absence.

To lead and influence your people effectively, you must invert the management pyramid, treat them as, in a sense, your personal customers and become curious about what makes them tick as individuals. You must start gathering all the information you can about what they want and need. In a managerial situation, you will sometimes have to guide, correct or even discipline these people, as well as inspire them, and you will need all this background knowledge for that, too. Again, remember that human behaviour really is purposeful.

If people have to change their behaviour, and cannot be shifted just by asking, you need to discover what payoffs they are getting out of continuing in the old ways. What does the unchanged behaviour do for them that makes them so loath to leave it behind? Everyone knows that people often continue with habits and behaviours that they keep telling others they don't want to do. But if the smoking or overeating or being self-critical is not understood as being a means to one or many ends, the outright clash between policy and performance will be a complete mystery. The smoker may get a feeling of confidence; the comfort eater may be looking for love in the fridge; the overly self-critical person may enjoy his Woody Allen persona in social situations, but find it hard to switch off when there is no audience. Each of these individuals may, however, have completely different motives that an outsider could never guess. But they will all be doing what they are doing for reasons that give them a payoff on some level.

If you are curious and careful to acknowledge people's individuality, while gleaning all the information you can about the motives that drive their behaviour, you will be able to move easily between the different roles required of you. Inspiring, planning, coaching, delegating, steering, instructing and correcting all make different demands and present different challenges. If you can combine them all, you are a true manager. If you can learn to excel in each of these roles, you will earn your recognition as a leader.

In a Nutshell   **Leading, Chunking and Delegating**

- **From managing to leading: increase your influence:**
  - Leadership benefits both the organisation and the people who are led.
  - The New Manager needs to be a leader.

- How do you lead? How do you want to lead?
- Do you give yourself credit for successes and treat yourself generously when results aren't perfect?

- **You're a leader, but how do you do it?**
  - To lead, you must influence people so that it engages their hearts and minds.
  - How do you enlist the co-operation of others?
  - Are you leading, or are you manipulating?
  - Leaders are careful to maintain linkage between what their people put in and the rewards they get.

- **You need to communicate on many different levels:**
  - Think about ambitious, long-term goals, but also what needs to be done on Monday morning.
  - Learn to recognise how individuals feel comfortable receiving information.

- **The overview and the detail:**
  - Recognise there are different chunk sizes. To explore, ask 'What have you been doing today?'
  - Those who give out information in bullet points also need to receive it in condensed format.
  - Small-chunk detail specialists need to edit material to suit the people they are talking to.
  - 30 seconds on the stairs or 30 minutes in an office? Relevance keeps people's attention.

- **The meaning of a communication is the response it triggers:**
  - The bullet-point person assumes everyone would do the same.
  - Leaders must operate effectively at both levels and move easily between them.

- **The magic of chunking:**
  - 7 ± 2 bits of information – between five and nine is most

people's limit.

– Learn to chunk raw data down to a size that works for you.

- **Stepping up the chunk sizes:**
  - 'What is this an example of?'
  - 'What could this be a part of?'
  - Pacing and leading: meet people on their home ground and lead them to a different perspective.
  - Always press farther than you think stepping up will go – it can usually be pushed to five steps or more.
  - It is useful to jolt your own thinking out of a rut.

- **Go to meet small-chunkers at their level of detail:**
  - 'What would be an aspect of this?'
  - 'What is a specific example of X?'
  - 'What is a part of this?'
  - Practise stepping down at least five levels.
  - Talk or ask about figures, specifications, dates, technicalities. Show you can and do think like them.

- **Small-chunkers hate deciding with incomplete data.**

- **Big-chunkers may be hazy about hurdles to overcome and resources needed for implementation.**

- **Where do you fit in?**
  - The big picture can mean you're weak on operational implementation.
  - If you are very small-chunk-oriented, you may find it difficult to delegate.

- **The first step in delegation is self-delegation:**
  - Give issues incubation time to allow unconscious creativity a chance.
  - Einstein said we use one-tenth of our brains, so there's still

room for limitless unconscious activity.

– Every brief you give automatically goes through self-delegation, because your brain is listening in.

- **Living with risks and learning from mistakes:**
  – Trust people to take risks, back their judgements and make errors.
  – Signal that learning lessons is approved of, while covering tracks or shifting blame is not.
  – How a manager responds to mistakes is a key factor in the team's success.
  – People don't come to work intending to do a bad job and make themselves feel awful.
  – Why do you go to work? Try to list *everthing* you get out of going to work.

- **Be curious about what makes your people tick:**
  – When you have to guide, correct and discipline them, you'll want this background knowledge.
  – They will all be doing what they do for reasons that give a payoff on some level.
  – Inspiring, planning, coaching, delegating, instructing and correcting all make different demands.
  – Be alert to people's individuality and you can move easily between roles.

Chapter 11
Catalysts for Creativity

'You must still have a spark of chaos inside you, to be able to give birth to a dancing star.'

(Friedrich Nietzsche, 1892)

➡ HOW TO TRAIN YOUR BRAIN TO CREATE MORE POSSIBILITIES

Anybody *can* be creative, we are always being told. And it's absolutely true. But that's not saying much, as long as that potential is regarded as dormant and hard to access. What is far more significant is that everybody actually *is* creative – and shows it every single day, whether the proof is recognised or not.

We may not go through our lives painting, sculpting, composing or writing plays or novels, nor even inventing gadgets, creating advertising campaigns or devising new software packages. But there are clear, identifiable signs of our creativity that can be pinpointed every day. We make jokes or playful comments about what is going on in our world. We fantasise about what we'd like to happen to us or imagine ourselves whisked away to a life of idleness on a tropical beach. We can hardly open our mouths to speak – especially in a rich and allusive language like English – without talking in conscious or unconscious metaphors. And, each night, we dream dreams as compelling as Spielberg, as weird as Dali, as lurid as Tarantino, as tense as Hitchcock, and as action-packed as Tom and Jerry.

By waking up and forgetting almost all of this unique and vivid dreamwork, we throw away enough ideas each night to keep Hollywood in business for years. That is how we are, all of us.

Creativity is there all the time. It is easy, spontaneous, effortless, abundant, and an entirely natural part of being human. You don't need to try; you just need to be. Yet people are often demoralised by low self-esteem when it comes to creativity. And it is all too easy to lose sight of the difference between creativity and originality.

If you think that you must be original to be creative, you are going to spend a lot of time being unnecessarily hard on yourself. Chaucer stole from Boccaccio and Petrarch, and Shakespeare helped himself to Holinshed. Einstein, whose Theory of Relativity is generally recognised as one of the supreme examples of human creativity, was directly indebted to Michelson and Morley's experiments in the 1880s and to the ideas of Ernst Mach. 'The work of the individual is so bound up with that of his scientific contemporaries,' he said, 'that it appears almost as an impersonal product of his generation.' Even Leonardo da Vinci's drawings of a possible design for a helicopter – 450 years ahead of its time – were not dreamt up out of the blue, but derived from his observations of sycamore seeds. Leonardo's genius, in this instance, lay in translating the germ of an idea across from the world of nature into the realm of technology. He recognised a parallel between the aerodynamic lift produced by a twirling seed case and the upward force that would have to be produced by mechanical means if humankind were to achieve the dream of being able to fly.

This ability to make connections between apparently unrelated objects and situations, to see equivalencies that may hardly exist and to carry ideas across from one domain to another, is the primary vehicle for human creativity. Association is the thief of time, in that it is always offering up one distraction after another and does not take you in a straight line to where you need to be. But it is also the true mother of invention. Associative thinking opens up pathways in the brain that were not there before, leaving a trace, a memory, that ensures that your thought, once conceived, will not become unthought again. You may think you have forgotten it, or half-remember and have it on the tip of your tongue, but once the idea has existed, the connection has been forged.

➡ THE POWER OF ASSOCIATIVE THINKING

Associative thinking knows no bounds and has no sense of propriety. It starts spontaneously and usually runs riot until you consciously decide to stop day-dreaming, pull yourself together and try to concentrate on something specific. It searches avidly, restlessly, for connections between the most unlikely objects and throws up a constant barrage of loopy ideas that appear totally unrelated to the matter in hand. Yet it is the very stuff of imagination and creativity and arguably the secret of how we get close to other people's experience, as well. When you ask what people have been doing and they start telling you about their Alpine holidays, you begin to remember a similar holiday you once had. You may re-experience how you felt and what it was like on the ski slopes. But when they tell you about being nervous in the cable car, your brain may jump to an entirely different holiday, when you were at Disney World in Florida and feeling apprehensive about the Space Mountain ride. As the brain flicks from one connection to the next, it combines breathtaking egocentricity with astonishing associative ingenuity. Its favourite line is 'Ah, this is like something that happened to me'. It needs a certain minimum amount of stimulation to feed off. But once that is provided, it will batten on to every scrap of justification it can find for connecting A with B – and with apple, aardvark, A1 quality, A-level exams, A4 paper, A–Z street guides, the A23 trunk road, Duke Ellington's train, ABCs, dates after Christ, going missing without leave, cashpoint machines, consumer credit rates and any other business. That's brains for you. Start them up and you never know where they'll go.

Because the brain works in this wild, chaotic, inspired way to provide us with the daily supply of associations and ideas we need, overspecialisation is one of the enemies of creativity. When people narrow down to a highly focused way of thinking about a highly specialised area, this can lead to tunnel vision, a condition that is often marked by the use of phrases such as 'There is no alternative'. In this type of situation, the range of possibilities that can ever be contemplated is limited by an oversimplified world-view. Poverty of stimulation means paucity of ideas. Brains need to be fed – not with improving books, necessarily, but with experience, talk, stimulation and input of all kinds. Unlike our poor lame-duck computers, where garbage in equals garbage out, the mighty brain can vacuum up any old nonsense, merge it in unholy associations with great thoughts from Plato and Dr Spock and a phrase or two from a Celine Dion song and come up with ... anything from total garbage to a practical suggestion for solving an engineering problem at work.

➡ WHO MADE UP THAT DREAM OF YOURS?

This is how we function during the day, when we are ostensibly under conscious control. At night, the gloves are off and creativity rules our inner world. For about 90 minutes, or even as much as two hours, each night, we will be in a very different state. We will be in dream sleep, also known as REM sleep, because of the darting rapid eye movements that accompany it. We are right inside our own Hollywood epics, watching and reacting to everything that happens around us, caught up in all that's going on and only saved from acting out our dreams by the fact that our muscles are switched off and paralysed throughout each bout of REM sleep.

Whether we remember them or not, we usually have about five dreams each night, each of them an entirely original creation, spontaneously generated by the brain for the occasion. So that's five premieres a night, seven nights a week, 52 weeks a year. By the time you are 30, that makes some 55,000 original dreams, and they are all your own work. In each of them, you have been the director, lead actor or narrator, scriptwriter, cinematographer, casting director, stunt co-ordinator, special effects supervisor, sound recordist and editor. You have plotted the stories, manipulated the characters and arranged the chase sequences and love scenes to thrill and engross you. You have undoubtedly managed to panic and terrify yourself, excite and amuse yourself and reproduce, at one time or another, every emotion and sensation you have ever felt in your waking life.

Your creativity runs riot every night of your life, rumbustious and amoral, uncensored by the codes and conventions of the waking world and uninhibited by any thoughts about whether or not you are an ideas person. Perhaps you are not. Perhaps this great outpouring of images and feelings isn't really you. But it is hard to imagine where else it can all have come from, other than inside your head. So if it isn't the you that you think you are, perhaps it's you who are not you. Dreams can be a catalyst for change, even when you can't remember any of the details and content. Just realising how natural creativity is and how much of it is surging around inside all of us can begin to change the way you perform when you put your suit on.

If you do remember your dreams when you wake up, try jotting down a couple of words to remind you of them, or mention the content briefly to your partner. Without something to jog your memory, they will soon be filed and forgotten. But if you can refer back to them two or three days later, or when the problem that has been on your mind surfaces again, you may be surprised to find that there is some association or symbolic connection that links the dream to the world. This is not a matter of easily-caricatured 'Freudian symbols' – guns, sports cars, and trains and tunnels – that would, allegedly, mean the same to everybody, but personal symbols and metaphors that might be of help to you.

If you look back at a dream and think 'Is there some way this could be telling me something about my problem?', you actually get two bites at the cherry. If the dream has no relevance at all, some near-random association with one of the elements in it may, while you are reviewing it, prompt an idea that could be useful. And there is always the chance that your subconscious may have been cleverer than you thought and may have constructed a narrative metaphor as a disguised way of telling you something you didn't want to hear ('Oh, I see now – perhaps the dog that chased me somehow represents the Inland Revenue'). Because we can't engage them at will, the resources available to us through our nightly investment in dreaming are mysterious and sometimes disturbing, but that does not mean that they don't exist.

The other daily creative routine we all share is day-dreaming, the much-maligned halfway house between wakefulness and sleeping. Everyone day-dreams, though bosses, teachers and parents often talk as if we shouldn't. The alternative reality of a day-dream is always less complete and absorbing than a full-scale dream. The muscular paralysis that goes with REM sleep is also missing, though the exaggerated, startled jump people give when disturbed in a day-dream tells you just how captivated they were by their imagination. The narrative logic of day-dreams can certainly be just as extraordinary and just as unpredictable as that of dreams, though, understandably, its origin is more likely to be rooted in the situation from which you slip off into your day-dream. Because of this combination of disinhibited thinking and a starting point that is related to the here and now, day-dreams can be especially useful in suggesting new approaches to problems. Both dreams and day-dreams offer access to certain kinds of creativity and mental processing beyond our ordinary, everyday thinking. They allow connections to be made that would not normally arise. But seeking inspiration in a dream is a hit and miss affair, at best, and not one you can usually attempt while you are at work. What is needed is a set of techniques you can use in the office to harness this same latent creativity and to make new connections and associations.

➡ USE PEOPLE'S METAPHORS TO UNLOCK THEIR CREATIVITY

The aim is to find ways of looking at your organisation and the challenges of your job from new angles and without the normal preconceptions about how things should be done. Making yourself and your colleagues talk about things in different terms, changing the language and metaphors you use, is one surprisingly effective way of doing this.

If you simply ask 'What is this organisation like, and in what way?', you will immediately push people into making connections and comparisons and recognising parallels with other situations, because they will be led to answer in some sort of simile or metaphor. Some of the reactions will be helpful, some trite. 'It's like a cheetah: swift, lean and purposeful', might be good to hear. 'It's like a golfer who can get onto the green, but never sink the vital putt' is rather more typical. And there are sometimes replies that paint quite a detailed symbolic picture of the organisation's strengths and weaknesses. 'This firm's like a 1950s Chevrolet – huge engine, huge fins and lots of chrome, but lousy steering and no protection at all in a crash,' one manager told us.

Once you have collected people's impressions and imagery, you can follow up with a set of more specific questions that build on this to provoke new ideas and promote new perspectives. 'Right,' you may say, 'If it's like an American car from the 1950s, what follows from that? What does that make possible for us? What does being like that stop us from doing that we ought to be doing?' This should open the way to genuinely fruitful discussion. The vague associative connection that generated the image of the Chevrolet in the first place will have been triggered by some perceived parallels between, say, the car's overstated fins and the company's flashy advertising campaigns. There may be parallels, too, based on the mismatch between the powerful R&D work that forms the company's engine and drives it forward and the apparent absence of anyone in the driving seat with a clear idea of how to keep it pointing in the right direction. However flip or facetious the imagery people offer, it is always worth dwelling on each answer for a while, to see where it might have come from and what the grain of truth in it might be.

If you feel the members of your group would be happy to go along with a slightly less matter-of-fact approach, you could try the guided metaphor tack. Try asking 'If this organisation were an animal, what animal would it be?', or 'If this firm were a piece of furniture, what would it be?' Again, you may get some flippant or sardonic answers. But you may also stumble across some ways of looking at the company that shed completely unexpected light on its strengths and weaknesses. Guided metaphors can be a quick and lighthearted way of persuading a group to focus on quite serious business matters. There will be many cases, though – particularly in the higher echelons of management – where it is not appropriate for the people involved to feel that they are taking part in a metaphor-hunting exercise. But there is often no need for this to be made explicit.

Example

The senior management team of one major British corporation was grappling with business process re-engineering on a grand scale, trying to create new structures for the twenty-first century and becoming bogged down in a mass of procedural wrangling. A meeting to resolve the impasse had broken up in disarray after four hours and everyone involved was fearful that reconvening the same group would only produce the same perplexing lack of progress. In an attempt to break the deadlock, Ian McDermott was called in as a facilitator. Following the principles of pacing and leading, he began by meeting the directors and managers on what they could all recognise as uncontroversial common ground, with a summary of what needed to be achieved – preceded by a nod in the direction of the procedural mindset that was clearly so dear to some of the participants. 'I understand that a whole set of new structures and processes need to be clarified and implemented,' he said. 'But it would be useful to be clear about what kind of organisation you are trying to create and how that will differ from the way the company is now. So I would like each person here today to think about one question. If you were to describe your existing organisation, what would you say it was like?'

Couched in these terms, the question was perfectly acceptable to this heavyweight group, which included main board directors, though it was actually an outright invitation to indulge in the fanciful business of dreaming up highly subjective metaphors. The most useful response to the question was an image that was recognised as appropriate by most of the people in the group: the image of a Cunarder, a luxury liner of the 1930s. As people warmed to the task of exploring this metaphor, the comments that came out where extremely revealing: 'The ship's plates and rivets are still sound, but the passengers she used to carry don't seem to be around much anymore.' 'She's big, strong and in danger of being empty.' 'And it's hard to see who is on the bridge.' 'You can see figures moving around in there, but the windows on the bridge are salted up, so you can't really see who's at the wheel.' This kind of insight, from directors and senior managers, is something that would have been unlikely to emerge in the course of normal debate, not least because several of the people in the room bore personal responsibility for the company's failure to move with the times. The image of the luxury liner provided a route for people to say what needed to be said and helped the group understand what purpose the introduction of the new structures and procedures was serving.

➡ CURIOUSER AND CURIOUSER

The ability to persuade, coax or ambush people into thinking in metaphorical terms, in order to unleash their creativity, is a skill the New Manager consciously cultivates. It is important at all levels of management, but becomes particularly significant for senior managers concerned with strategic thinking and the development of the corporate vision. Because of the strangely romantic notion that creativity is too fragile to be pursued with any deliberate intent, managers are supposed to have brilliantly fresh ideas with no knowledge of what is most likely to facilitate their arrival. Yet there are tried and tested ways of increasing the chances that you will be able to generate the bright ideas and unexpected solutions you need, when you need them. One ground rule, for example, is to foster and feed your own sense of curiosity.

If you are not curious about people, events and ideas, it is harder to see things differently and make the original and unexpected mental associations that lead to breakthroughs. It is quite possible to make a conscious investment in whetting your curiosity and in seeking out mental stimulation.

> Try making a written list of six things or topics you have always been curious about. They can be anything at all. One might be a question you have never had properly answered. One might be a subject that always catches your attention when it is featured in TV documentaries. Other items on your list could be broad general categories ('people', 'languages', 'sex', 'Asia' or 'how medicines work', perhaps), or activities that have a mysterious attraction for you, such as Morris dancing, archaeology, mountaineering or lace-making. When you have compiled your personal list, ask yourself: 'What is it about these things that makes me curious about them?'

It's worth spending a few minutes going over the list. Are there any common themes underlying these areas of interest and fascination? Suppose you started getting curious about other things in this same way. How would work be different then? Whenever you choose not to take familiar things for granted, you open up the possibility of change and creativity. Simple, childlike questions – 'Why do we always take this route?', 'What would happen if we did something completely different?', and 'Who says there's only one way to do the job?' – can jolt you and your colleagues out of the rut of lazy, routine thinking and spark new ideas and approaches.

Being curious makes you interested. And being interested makes you interesting – a factor that can have direct payoffs in career terms. When candidates for a demanding management position are being compared, there is always a strong prejudice in favour of the more interesting people, subjective though that judgement is. People who are curious, interested and interesting come across as bigger, broader people – and, therefore, the sort of powerful, flexible, open-minded individuals every company wants to see in key positions in times of unpredictable change.

At the very least, signs of an absorbing outside interest can have an important bearing on the way people respond to you.

Example

We worked for some years with a main board director of one of Britain's top corporations, an edgy, reserved man with a brilliant technical background but a chilling manner and a ruthless reputation. Those who feared him saw only the cold technocrat. But those who worked for him were surprisingly loyal and found the key to a more human side of his character in his passion for sailing small boats in rough waters. For his staff, the sailing was an important antidote to his grave demeanour, a reassuring indication that there was warmth, fallibility and creativity beneath the icy surface.

What you do and what you are known for doing help to define who you are perceived to be. So it makes sense, for both personal and career reasons, to follow where your curiosity leads. Find out about the subjects that catch your attention, develop your hobbies and leisure interests and actively pursue the things you find intellectually stimulating. If you find it mentally stretching to go rock climbing or visit new places or learn Brazilian dance forms or read about food or philosophy or the origins of the universe, do it. Do them all, because it's unlikely that you will only have one hobbyhorse that engages your interest. Apart from enjoying yourself and saving your brain from death by atrophy, you will be making a significant investment in your ability to perform creatively at work. And there may just come a day when you find that you have a shared interest with someone who is a key player in your future career.

In a Nutshell   Catalysts for Creativity

- **Don't think you must be original to be creative:**
  - Creativity is about connections, carrying ideas across from here to there.
  - Brains need to be stimulated.

- **Who made up that dream of yours?**
  - 55,000 dreams by the time you're 30 – and you've directed all of them.
  - Make a note so your dream isn't lost.
  - Your subconscious may find a metaphor to tell you something.

- **Managers need techniques to harness creativity.**

- **Let people's metaphors unlock their creativity.**

- **What is this organisation like – and in what way?**
  - What follows from that?
  - What does that make possible for you?
  - What does being like that stop you from doing that you ought to be doing?

- **Use the catalyst of guided metaphor:**
  - If this organisation were an animal, what animal would it be?

- **Curiouser and curiouser:**
  - Feed your own curiosity.
  - See things differently and you'll see new associations.

- **Make a list of six things you have always been curious about:**

- What is it that makes you curious about them?
- How would work be different if you were this curious about other things?

- **Being interested makes you interesting – and that has payoffs:**
  - Pursue the thing or things you find stimulating. Do it. Do them all.

Chapter 12
The Power of Benchmarking

'Begin with another's to end with your own.'

(Baltasar Gracian, 1647)

➡ HOW TO DO BETTER THAN YOU EVER THOUGHT POSSIBLE

Done well, benchmarking is pure NLP. It is the careful and detailed study of excellence, a way of thinking that is entirely concerned with the pursuit of what works, rather than the avoidance of what doesn't. After all, the real secret of success is learning how to repeat it. The only way that can be done in practice is to systematise and refine the processes you use to achieve results, so that their impact and effects can be predicted with a reasonable amount of certainty. It is widely recognised that benchmarking can help you do this in business. It is not so widely recognised that the same principles can be brought to bear in the effort to improve your personal performance. In this chapter, we want to give you some tools for operational benchmarking, first at an organisational level and then for you as a person.

Traditionally, business has tended to be hypnotised by history and, in many cases, suprisingly inward-looking. The future has been seen as a rather wilful and unruly mirror of the past, which, if properly brought under control, can be persuaded to yield the same as before plus, say, 10 per cent. Incremental improvement has been accepted as the goal. It is only when you look around and see that there are other organisations that are doing the same sort of things as you, but doing them vastly better, that the realisation dawns that big, radical, unnerving, fundamental changes may be needed. Benchmarking may provide the ideas and processes that can make this happen. It starts with the question 'Who does this much better than we do?', and follows up with a serious study of the processes that make this exceptional performance possible.

In searching for the role models that can teach you the secrets of best possible practice, it is important to look beyond the boundaries of your own industry. Industry norms and accepted 'best practice' are always determined by the old guard. If you are planning to excel, you need to be able to draw useful parallels between the processes and functions of your business and those that apply in completely different industry sectors. Some of the most successful instances of benchmarking have revolved round this kind of inter-industry cross-fertilisation.

Examples

- One American airline reasoned that every minute it kept its planes on the ground at an airport was a minute's revenue down the drain. It looked for expertise in fast turnround procedures – and found it among the pit-stop crews at the Indianapolis 500 racetrack.

- When Xerox wanted to speed up its order picking and packing function, it discovered the role model it wanted in an international sportswear supplier's mail order operation, which was dealing with a similar task at three times the speed.

- NHS hospital trust managers enlisted the help of British Airways in a benchmarking exercise to improve operating theatre scheduling, after spotting that much of the process – with its bookings, cancellations, delays and no-shows – was comparable to BA's passenger handling procedures.

Lateral thinking is needed to break the habit of only looking at your competitors, but the effort can be immensely rewarding.

➡ MAKING AN INSPIRED CHOICE

Since this kind of lateral thinking is often hard to conjure up to order, it is helpful to have a procedure to start the ball rolling. We suggest you play the game of picking an industry as far away as possible from your own and pretending that you have already decided that this is where the answer to your problems lies. Choose a company within that field and say to yourself, as if you already knew the answer, but had forgotten: 'What were we going to learn from them?' So, if you are financial software developers, trying plumping for an oil company like BP or a consumer goods group like Unilever or for engineers like Bechtel or Brown & Root. If you make cardboard packaging, adopt the idea that you can learn from an ad agency like Saatchi or from Ford. If you're in retailing, try Zeneca or KPMG. Immediately discount any candidate that seems likely to have some sensible, logical relevance and work outwards from there.

When you have arbitrarily chosen a possible benchmarking model, stand back from your own company's problems and ambitions and think, in the abstract, about what your model is particularly good at. Leisure attractions, breweries and fast food companies are all skilled at predicting and responding to fluctuating demand. Banks, airlines and drug manufacturers all have highly developed quality assurance systems. Construction firms know all about project management, supermarket chains have the slickest distribution operations and phone companies have some of the most flexible billing systems around. In the course of this exercise, you will either identify some unexpected connection between your company's situation and the potential model's expertise or suddenly catch yourself thinking that this would have been a whole lot easier if you had chosen Company X. In which case, you simply switch horses and investigate the possibility of using Company X as your real role model in a proper, systematic benchmarking project.

➡ LOOK FOR THE POINT OF LEVERAGE

Benchmarking requires the co-operation of a successful company in an industry other than your own and it may be a challenge to persuade your potential partner to accept the intrusion that can be involved. That is a matter for negotiation. There will probably have

to be the possibility of some payoff for the firm being benchmarked, which could be based on linkage to some other desirable
deal between you, the supply of services on a barter basis or a
reciprocal arrangement where the other company benchmarks
some aspect of your organisation. In many cases, though, the fee
for co-operation in a benchmarking exercise will just be the
sharing of detailed information gleaned during the project. The
truth is that many successful organisations do not consciously
know how they do it or exactly why their methods are so
exceptionally effective, which can make it difficult for them to
replicate or scale up their success. If the analytical outsider's view
that helps you learn also helps pin down what the benchmarked
operation is doing right, it may provide useful insights and save
many thousands of pounds in consultancy fees. Since many
managers have an almost pathological distrust of consultants, even
when they know there is consultancy work that urgently needs to
be done, this may be your strongest argument.

The other essential before beginning a benchmarking exercise is
to establish precisely what your own company does now. People
often think they know what happens on a daily or weekly basis,
when the practical reality is quite different. But unless you
examine your own organisation in enough detail to provide an
exact picture of current practice, you cannot possibly make useful
comparisons with other people's methods.

Once you have engaged the co-operation of a suitable partner
and uncovered the reality of your present practices, the benchmarking project itself can get under way. The key qualities that are
needed, apart from diplomacy and a tactful awareness that you are
stepping into other people's space, are a sharp eye, an open mind
and a determination to watch exactly what does happen, rather
than what people say happens, without any attempt to interpret
your observations until all the facts are known. It is worth bearing
in mind that it will usually be the *process* that provides interesting
lessons for the future, rather than the content.

Remember, too, that you do not need to accept the methods or
approach of even the most successful benchmarked organisation
wholesale. If you can see brilliantly simple ideas being put into
practice alongside some less inspired methods that you feel are
holding back the overall performance – making it just good, when

it could be astounding – you are free to pick and choose. Take careful note of both aspects, because it is possible that you have misunderstood something about what's going on. If you try to emulate successful performance by replicating what seems obviously good and it doesn't work, you may want to look again at the contribution being made by what seemed to you to be not so admirable. You are looking for what works. When you compare and contrast your benchmarking target company with your own organisation, you are searching for the crucial point of leverage, the difference that makes the difference, in order to be able to improve your results. If you can find it and import the lessons into your own operations, you will gain the ability to enhance your performance on a consistent and repeatable basis.

➡ HOW TO BENCHMARK YOURSELF

If benchmarking is seen as a generic approach to the search for improvement through the study of relevant models of excellence, it makes sense to look at your own 'personal bests' and see what can be learnt from them. Many people are past masters at noticing what they are not so good at and recalling with acute clarity the times when they did not do well at whatever they were attempting. Far fewer have developed the skill of noticing what they are doing that is working well, so that they can systematically recreate the conditions for repeating their success.

Think, for a minute, of three occasions at work when you did something outstandingly well. The examples do not need to be spectacular and they do not have to have been noticed by anyone else. Nor do they need to represent perfect 10s, with no room for future improvement. Just pick three instances in which you can feel rightly proud of what you accomplished. Now ask yourself, in each case, 'What did I do?' and 'Can I pinpoint what made the difference that time?' If you are going to improve your performance, to match and beat your personal best, you need to pay close attention to your own best practice and to start noticing what really works for you. When you have singled out the factors that made the difference – the qualities, skills and behaviours that you were deploying to produce this success – think of other times when things didn't go so well. Would it have made a useful and positive difference if those qualities could have been present? Would everything automatically have been rosy? Probably not. But wouldn't it, at the very least, have been easier to handle the sticky situations that you were involved in?

One of the most purposeful career moves you can make is to get into the habit of doing a regular personal performance audit and making it a matter of policy to focus hard on what is working, rather than obsessively gnawing away at what isn't. In particular, whenever a project or an interview or presentation goes magically well, you should consciously examine your memory of it afterwards and analyse what you did to achieve this result. But even without such outstanding examples, a weekly review of your lesser successes and the things you feel good about will reveal an increasing number of examples of competence, and even elegance, in your day-to-day performance. In this way, you can be your own coach in this area and encourage yourself to build up what amounts to a reference database of your own best practice. Experience has always been the greatest teacher. You can let it guide you and let the growing collection of reference experiences serve to validate your capacity to surprise yourself and surpass the presumed limits of your ability. There is usually plenty of room for this sort of surprise, because there are not many of us who consistently err on the side of overestimating our capabilities at work.

For most of the human race, an excess of modesty is the more likely failing. Which brings us on to the single most provocative exercise in the whole of this book. In a moment, we are going to ask you to write down a list of 20 things that you are really good at. And you, predictably, are going to think that you cannot do it, because 20 is just far too many and you don't have that many talents. And we are going to contradict you, because we have done this exercise many times before and everybody – possibly with a little prompting – but *everybody*, gets there in the end.

These skills and talents and aptitudes and knacks and competencies and quirky fortes do not have to be work-related or particularly unusual. By the time you have linked more than a handful of them in a list, you'll be well on your way to defining yourself as a unique individual. They may include informal skills that cannot lead to qualifications, like having a good telephone manner or a knack for spotting market niches, or being good with children, or being a strong swimmer or able to cook Chinese food. If you can speak French, tell stories, do sums in your head, write advertising copy, stitch wounds, drive a heavy goods vehicle, ski, find long words at Scrabble, conduct job interviews, play the oboe and argue the hind leg off a donkey, your life experiences have obviously dealt you an interesting hand and you should put all of them down.

Do it now. Take a couple of minutes to jot down your catalogue of 20 abilities, bearing in mind that you are creating a list that reflects a surprising amount about your tastes, history and individuality and has never seen the light of day in this form before. This is an instant CV that may well say more about you than any career résumé you have ever sent off. Copy it later today and file the copy away in a safe place. Sooner or later, you will want to refer to it again.

➡ REMEMBER THE MILLION-DOLLAR MERMAID

Just considering your list can be quite startling and thought-provoking. But the next step is to think of the ideal job for the person this list describes – and if one doesn't exist, to invent it. Designing a job specification based on a selection of these skills and aptitudes may sound like a fatuous exercise, but it is something a surprising number of people, including household names in the entertainment industry, have managed to do.

Example

There was the American swimming champion with high hopes of international success, until the war put a stop to the 1940 Olympics. She had a shapely body, a pleasant voice, a reasonably pretty face, a great deal of ambition and, of course, the ability to swim like an eel, but there was no existing job spec that seemed to call for this combination of attributes. The new career she invented out of the blue for herself was that of wet film star, or amphibian actress, and Esther Williams pursued it successfully for a decade or more, taking the lead in a number of rather specialised and very popular movies, with titles such as *Dangerous When Wet* and *The Million-Dollar Mermaid*.

If you could define a previously undreamt-of career for yourself, in the light of your talents list, what would it be like?

Have you just identified what you should really be doing with your working life? Have you just received confirmation that you are on the right track? Or does the job that would combine and exploit your personal range of talents simply not exist? If that is the case now, it may not necessarily always be so. So much is changing in the world of business that this peculiar sort of job might well come into being at some time in the future. There are many careers available today that simply did not exist even seven or eight years ago, such as Web site designer, railway entrepreneur, or English supermarket manager in Calais. There will be comparable opportunities in a few years' time, though we can't even begin to guess yet what they might be. If you carry with you a realistic awareness of the full range of your own talents – both professional and 'non-vocational' – you will be more alert to emerging possibilities that may dovetail in unexpected ways with your personal list.

The other, more immediate, payoff from creating this list is the effect it can have on your present job. By acknowledging and recognising all your talents, without false modesty, you can equip yourself to play to your strengths. When a new project comes up that you can choose to volunteer for or leave to someone else, measure its demands against the list you have just made and base your decision on that. The more elements on your list it might engage, the more likely you are to be the right person to do it. The more of you you can work into your work, the more indispensable you become. It makes life at work more interesting and fulfilling. It makes you more irreplaceable, and less downsizeable when times are hard.

Just being aware of how many talents you have and valuing the breadth of resources they give you will encourage you to behave more confidently and decisively as a manager. But, like the company that looks outside to acquire new ideas and approaches through benchmarking, you may recognise that there are qualities or skills you need that you are unlikely to gain from books or training courses. So can benchmarking techniques be made to work between individuals on a one-to-one basis? The answer is a definite yes – though personal benchmarking can operate on a wide variety of levels, with or even without the knowing co-operation of the benchmarked person.

➡ SPEND TIME IN THE COMPANY OF EXCELLENCE

Benchmarking formed one of the major dynamics in the age-old system of master craftsmen and their apprentices. The boy would be bound apprentice to the craftsman, usually for a period of seven years (though one London guild, the saddlers, demanded ten years) and would receive board and lodging, but no wages. The old man would teach the boy the skills, traditions and unwritten rules of the trade, gradually delegating more and more challenging parts of the task, year by year, until the apprentice was straining at the leash to be allowed to take full responsibility for a job. Only when the boy was so full of confidence, ambition and determination that he was convinced he could match or outdo the master was he finally allowed to show what he could achieve. By the time the training was complete, the boy had absorbed so much of the senior man's approach, habits and attitudes, as well as his technical skills, that it was impossible to tell what had been learnt by instruction and what had transferred across by a kind of osmosis. This is an extreme instance of learning by example. The people you recognise as having the management skills you want may not wish to have you following them round for seven years – and, besides, they may have weaknesses, alongside their strengths, which you would certainly not wish to acquire as part of the bargain.

On the other hand, everyone knows from experience that people who work or live together tend to adopt each other's mannerisms, speech patterns, modes of thought and working practices, consciously or unconsciously. If you want to become really good at something, you can learn what you need to know by spending time with people who can do it superbly. The art of personal benchmarking is to discover the positive and relevant parts of their behaviour and emulate them with care and precision, discarding what is clearly not contributing to the desired result. We all know that the dog and its owner grow more alike over the years, but the relationship would not be beneficial in either direction if they each adopted too much of the other's lifestyle. Nevertheless, it will not always be clear what is going on and what aspects of behaviour are generating the success you want to replicate. Patient observation is necessary, combined with an attitude of curiosity, rather than judgement. Even when you talk to the experts you hope to learn from, bear in mind that what people think they do and what they actually do, especially under pressure, can be very different. Watching attentively, registering the fine detail and asking a lot of questions can help you establish what is really going on and put you on the road towards matching the excellence you have identified in your benchmarking model.

It is surprising how often there is very little separating the average from the outstanding. As you search for the little differences that make all the difference, you will realise that excellence may not be far away. Like the casting vote in the Israeli Knesset or that last parcel of shares that tips the balance in a hostile takeover, the decisive factor can often be something easily ignored or taken for granted. In the context of business practices and management techniques, it may be routines that are so familiar and unspectacular that no one thinks to mention them. But all successful organisations are doing something right and many have multiple lessons to offer, as have the people that make them tick. Benchmarking is the key to making that conscious and unconscious expertise your own.

In a Nutshell   The Power of Benchmarking

- **How to do better than you ever thought possible:**
  - The real secret of success is learning how to repeat it.
  - Use lateral thinking and look beyond your own industry.

- **Making an inspired choice:**
  - Pick an industry far from your own and pretend you already know the answer's there.
  - What were we going to learn from them?

- **Look for the point of leverage:**
  - The fee for co-operation is usually the sharing of detailed information.
  - Establish precisely what your own company does now.

- **Watch what happens, rather than what people say happens:**
  - It's usually *process* that offers lessons, rather than content.
  - Look for what works.

- **How to benchmark yourself:**
  - Think of three occasions at work when you did something outstandingly well.
  - Ask 'What did I do?' and 'Can I pinpoint what made the difference?'
  - Do a regular personal performance audit and review your successes.
  - Build up a reference database of your own best practice.

- **List 20 things you are good at:**
  - This is an instant CV – copy it and file the copy.

- **Remember the million-dollar mermaid:**
  - What's the ideal job for the person your list describes?
  - If it doesn't exist, invent it.

- **Personal benchmarking can work on different levels.**

- **Spend time in the company of excellence:**
  - Register the fine detail.
  - All successful organisations and people are doing something right.
  - Benchmarking helps you make that expertise your own.

Chapter 13
Expect the Unexpected

'Nothing is permanent but change.'
(Heraclitus, c. 500 BC)

➡ **YOU CAN'T CONTROL THE FUTURE ... BUT YOU CAN BE ON YOUR TOES AND READY FOR IT**

Change is everywhere these days, just as it was 2500 years ago, when Heraclitus waxed philosophical about it in ancient Greece. But there is a widespread fear and dread of change in offices and factories now that simply didn't exist in this form even a generation ago. Having seen their friends and colleagues lose jobs in the mass redundancies and downsizing of the early 1990s, people feel insecure, suspicious and wary of any sort of change. Yet there are some industries, such as computing, telecommunications and fast food catering, that have expanded and even accelerated their rate of growth in recent years, creating new jobs, new wealth and new prospects. The problem is that change – all change – is generally seen as threatening, as if what we had enjoyed in the recent past was a matchless golden era that could never be equalled by anything the future might hold.

Sometimes it seems as though we have all become small-C conservatives, convinced that all change is for the worse. But what would it be like if change simply ground to a halt? Imagine a situation where the nature of your job and your work commitments never changed at all, throughout a working life of 40 years or so. That would have been the lot of most of us in mediaeval times, when 'the rich man in his castle, the poor man at his gate' both knew their place and the poor man was dumb and helpless enough to put up with it. Change may mean insecurity and uncertainty, but it also means interest, excitement and the positive stimulus of new situations, ideas and people. So it is not change itself that is the challenge. It is more the fact that when things change around us as fast as our technologies and our society are doing now, we feel vulnerable and out of control.

➡ THE DICTATOR'S FALLACY

The trouble is, control does not work in the face of rapid and unpredictable change. As a matter of policy, the New Manager does not believe that banging one's head against brick walls, tilting at windmills and setting oneself up for heroic failures is worth the effort. The best you can do is make sure you have the ability to manage the key elements, while allowing enough space for a fair amount of variation. Beyond this core, you need to understand what's going on, delegate what has to be done and be prepared to change or adjust your plans, possibly several times, in the light of developing situations.

As a prescription for survival, this does not sound especially revolutionary. But it contrasts dramatically with the observable reality in many British and American companies. Too many managers suffer from an intense desire to make sense of the world by controlling it. Their strategy for managing others and advancing their own careers is based on trying to control all the variables in each situation, usually by imposing a rigid system of rules. When carried to excess, it means they stifle initiative and inhibit the creativity of their people and end up doing – or at least deciding – everything themselves, meticulously micromanaging every detail. They become control freaks, addicted to control, but unable ever to get enough of it. Like the monstrous dictators of the twentieth century, from Lenin and Stalin to Hitler, Mussolini and Pol Pot, their behaviour springs from insecurity and a fundamental misunderstanding about how the world works. We call this the Dictator's Fallacy. It goes like this: 'If I can only gain more control, I'll finally be able to dictate the course of events.' It is a patently absurd proposition, but you can see it underlying the behaviour of many people – including, incidentally, many managers who are humane, well-meaning and anxious to be liked.

The reasoning that stems from this kind of belief is simple: 'I just need a bit more control and I'll be all right – my position will be secure and I can get what I want.' The sufferers' assumptions are based on fear that without this control over others, they will lose out, or even that other people will sneak up and do them down. And since all overcontrolled, repressive regimes, in business and politics, breed anxiety and resentment, the fear is not without foundation. When you add into the equation the fact that business performance is always at the mercy of the big external factors – the weather, interest and exchange rates, government policies, legislative change, forthcoming elections and consumer booms – it is clear that the very idea of control is an illusion. You can't out-control change.

What you can usefully do is understand and accommodate change as a necessary part of business life. Although our fear of the unexpected is always trying to tell us the challenge of change is a purely external matter, that is not true. The real challenge is internal. The question that matters, given the implacable, unavoidable nature of much external change, is how flexible, resourceful and creative you can be in the face of a change of circumstances, a new job description or location, departmental restructurings, downsizing or takeovers. What is happening is undeniably important. What you make of it is decisive. If you are flexible enough to find some good in the changes and turn them to advantage, there is a double benefit. Besides the initial advantage, you will re-establish your sense of being able to influence the course of events, rather than suffering the debilitating feeling of being swept powerlessly along with the stream.

It is considerably easier to recognise flexibility than to be flexible. But there are ways of consciously moving yourself towards greater flexibility and you can start by defining it by its opposite.

> Think of three people you consider to be absolute models of rigidity and inflexibility. Objective truth is not important here; it's what you see in them that counts. What is it about each of these three people that makes you feel they come across as so exceptionally rigid? Identify specific factors and award marks out of ten to each of your nominees in each of these categories.

Now think of three people whose flexibility you have noticed and admired and rate them out of ten in identical categories.

Compared with these two groups, picked and defined by you, where would you rate yourself on the same scales? How would you describe yourself?

➡ WOULD OTHER PEOPLE CALL YOU FLEXIBLE?

If you think you already count as remarkably flexible, that's excellent, though you should remember that everyone has areas in which they could still show more flexibility. Now, how would other people rate you? Do they think of you as a little too rigid and inflexible? Are you perceived as having a talent for handling the unexpected? If you are, you already possess one of the major attributes of the New Manager. Your people will be loyal to you and accept you as a genuine leader, because flexibility is one of the most important qualities a leader can demonstrate. People find it reassuring and inspiring to be led by someone who, if he or she doesn't know all the answers in advance, can make it up on the hoof and still get it right more often than not. For the people you manage, that is the ultimate guarantee that they will not be wrongfooted by change and asked to make heroically pointless sacrifices, on the lines of the Charge of the Light Brigade or the First Day of the Somme. Being flexible does not mean you don't have a position and it doesn't mean you won't fight to defend it. But it does give you more options about how to achieve your goals. The more inflexible you are, the fewer choices you have. Rigidity equals brittleness. And brittle things snap. In Japan and California, where skyscrapers have to coexist with the threat of abrupt change in the form of earthquakes, the tallest buildings are deliberately designed to move and flex to absorb seismic shocks without damage, though they do, of course, 'stand their ground', in the sense that they remain in the same place. As well as the spectacular, catastrophic change associated with earthquakes, they are also built to accommodate the unseen forces of subtler change, swaying in the breeze several feet out of the perpendicular.

When change is thrust upon us as a *fait accompli*, we tend to resent the feeling that we are not in control and immediately look on the gloomy side. It is a significant talent to be able to shift rapidly out of this mindset and begin to scan the new situation for the good it might bring. Forced relocations and mass redundancy programmes are always resented, and the changes they bring, undoubtedly disrupt people's established lifestyles. Yet many of the British financial services companies that have relocated from London to places such as Bristol, Swindon, Winchester, Reading and Leeds have found surprisingly high proportions of their managerial staff quite willing, on reflection, to accept generous relocation packages. The opportunity to move to parts of the country where they can now choose to live in rural bliss, within easy commuting distance of a job that will still pay a good salary, has persuaded many people that such uprooting need not always be negative.

Example

Downsizing programmes, like the repeated rounds of redundancies that enabled British Telecom to cut its payroll from almost 250,000 to less than half that, without any forced departures, can provide lump-sum payoffs that make thousands of people's dreams come true. For long-serving BT middle managers with extensive networks of contacts and every chance of lining up good jobs without too much delay, the opportunity to exit with dignity, bank £60,000 or £80,000 and join the ambitious newcomers in the telecommunications industry was a very substantial silver lining.

➡ DON'T LET FEAR STOP YOU IN YOUR TRACKS

There is actually far less 100 per cent bad news around than people tend to think. When the unexpected happens and your reaction is to see it negatively, ask yourself 'Who is this bad for?' The answer is seldom going to be that it is bad for everybody. So ask the appropriate sequence of questions:

- 'Who is this bad news good for?'
- 'Is there some way the benefit to them can become a benefit to me?'

- 'Does this mean that there is something I or we, as an organisation, should be doing to make the most of the changed situation?'

To take the most brutal of examples, the senior managers in a public company that has been the subject of a hostile takeover are invariably candidates for a brisk and unsentimental clearout. Everyone immediately fears the worst and it is usually inevitable that heads will roll, with a winnowing of board directors and direct reports as the new masters take control. On the other hand, this can create accelerated advancement opportunities for those managers that are left, since business continuity will absolutely require the presence of some experienced people with specific product, project and customer knowledge. In circumstances like this, the people who quickly reconcile themselves to the realities of the new situation can do well. Those, for example, who draw up practical submissions as to how the two organisations' structures and functions can be merged most effectively may well find themselves given the chance to put their proposals into action. In the old, comfortable, pre-takeover days, such an opportunity might still have been several years away. In a conservative company, where radical initiatives were not encouraged, it might never have come at all. The lesson is that times of change and turmoil create opportunities as well as disruption. Those who react fastest and most decisively, though they may be as apprehensive as all the rest, stand the best chance of finding some good in the situation.

The great danger, in an atmosphere of fear and change, is paralysis. If you are frozen into immobility, locked solid with terror like a rabbit in headlights, you are lined up to be crushed by the juggernaut of your fate. A small shot of fear may be stimulating – if it weren't for deadlines, how many journalists would ever sit down and write? – but there is all the difference in the world between the dose that sets the adrenalin surging and the brain racing and the incapacitating shock of full-scale panic. Fear builds on itself, because being afraid is a consuming, self-absorbed state. Being scared gives you even more to be scared about, because as you fixate on your fears, you can see fewer and fewer options. This, of course, is exactly the opposite of what is needed to handle the unexpected. You need to be able to stand back, take a cool look at all the implications of the new situation, positive and negative, and formulate a constructive, well-reasoned plan. Instead, if you once let your fear get the upper hand, you are likely to be digging yourself deeper and deeper into the pit of helpless despondency. The antidotes to fear are action – any action that changes your state is good news – and planning – any planning that takes your thinking beyond the immediate and daunting present. Walk, swim, talk, drive, visit a factory or go and sell someone something. Activate yourself and you'll activate the resources you need to bounce back.

Change does not always come in sweeping cataclysmic waves, as a merger, a takeover or an unexpected branch closure. Sometimes it creeps up slowly, as in the revolting boiled frog analogy Charles Handy and other management theorists refer to, which alleges that a frog placed in a pan of cold water over a low heat will fatally fail to react to the steady, incremental increase in temperature until it is too late. Sometimes change strikes with catastrophic force for one individual, while declining to touch the person next in line. If you are told to clear your desk and go, it hardly matters at the time that the rest of your colleagues still have jobs to come in for. The fear of change can be equally disruptive, whether the change involves companies, departments or just a single individual – and whether or not it is based on any real and imminent threat.

➡ LIST YOUR FIVE FEARS

We all have our fears and nightmares and it is sometimes useful to acknowledge them, with a view to exorcising some of their emotional power. A few of the most common work-based examples are fear of losing one's job, fear of not achieving recognition for good work, fear of being unfairly singled out for criticism, fear of boredom, and fear of just not being able to cope.

These are very broad, generic fears that could be made much more specific in any particular workplace. But the same basic themes recur in most companies. Are you aware of the fears that hover in the background of your own behaviour at work?

Try making a list of your five worst fears. When you have done it, see whether you can recognise how each of these five factors has intervened at one time or another to affect and limit your performance.

Example

One example of a relatively trivial fear running totally out of control was the case of a senior executive at a chemical engineering company we worked with. This man was desperate to win the approval of his boss and lived with real anxiety about the possibility of suffering rejection or disapproval. He worked hard and for long hours, volunteering for everything and taking on more than anyone could reasonably have been expected to cope with. Eventually the boss began to notice all this and withdraw slightly from the intensity of what was going on. Undaunted, the man worked more, harder, longer, until the boss grew irritated by his constant hyperactivity and the executive's wife became so used to his absence that she left home herself. The fear of disapproval that had been the motivation for good work in the first place had damaged his career prospects and blighted his marriage.

Yet this was one of those instances where a simple intervention is able to produce a remarkably profound change for the better. By inviting the client – an ambitious and intelligent man – to view the situation from outside, as if looking at a film, and describe what appeared to be happening between the characters in the movie, it was possible to help him see for himself what was driving the situation. Once he had a clear idea of what the problem was and how he was being controlled by his fear, he was perfectly capable of devising his own strategies to realign his behaviour with the goals that really mattered to him.

➡ IS YOUR PAST RUNNING YOUR PRESENT?

Though fear, like change, is always an emotional subject, it is important to recognise that fear comes in several different guises and varieties. Perhaps the most incapacitating, because it can seem impossible to combat with normal reason and intelligence, is the sort of fear that is a hangover from experiences long past. If your past is running your present, it is unlikely to make a good job of it. For example, it is obviously not unreasonable to be afraid of the prospect of being unemployed. If you are afraid of unemployment because your conscious mind has noticed that the company is downsizing and those around you keep receiving letters in ominous brown envelopes, the subject is bound to loom large in your thoughts. But if it is a long-standing fear based on your parents' tales of an austerity and privation you never knew, it may be completely unnecessary and unhelpful baggage that you do not need to carry with you into the twenty-first century. We know of at least two people who quite definitely live with this unnecessary fear – unnecessary because, in both cases, the individuals own their own well-established companies and do not have bosses to please, nor any serious reason to expect anything other than steady, modest expansion and total job security throughout the rest of their working lives.

When the past takes charge of the present, though, anything can happen. Many high-flying managers suffer either from fear of heights or fear of flying. We have come across others who cannot use lifts and several who cannot travel on the underground – Northern Line, Piccadilly Line, Paris Metro, New York subway or, increasingly significantly, Eurostar. These people do not usually wish to advertise their phobias, so they go to great lengths to skirt round the areas and activities that are likely to cause difficulties.

Example

Ian McDermott worked once with an executive coaching client who had a problem with the increased amount of international travelling his success made necessary. Whenever he made his whistle-stop trips around Europe, he used to insist on arranging all the logistics and booking every hotel himself, which cost him a great deal of time and effort, especially as he became involved in complicated telephone discussions with each hotel before confirming the reservation. His PA, naturally enough, wondered why he refused to delegate something as straightforward, dull and workaday as hotel bookings to her and concluded that he must have some lurid and unpleasant skeleton in the cupboard. His problem, in fact, was that he had to make sure every hotel room he went to had no window or had one that looked out onto a blank wall or an airshaft – anything but the wide, picturesque views the other hotel guests would want.

Using a particular NLP technique, he was able to pin this fear down to an incident in his early childhood when his mother had taken him for a walk across a new suspension bridge and held him up to look out over the valley below. The sensation of danger and vertigo had totally overwhelmed the boy and the man had carried the fear with him ever since. Simply knowing where the fear had come from did not, in itself, lift the burden. But once McDermott had used a fairly standard procedure known as the NLP Phobia Cure, the man was able to enjoy his travelling and delegate his hotel booking to anyone, without having to admit to a fear which he had always felt would be seen as a sign of weakness.

➡ DON'T GET STUCK FIGHTING THE LAST WAR

Like many fears and all phobias, this coaching client's fear was debilitating and unhelpful. But it had developed to serve a noble purpose – self-preservation in the face of danger. The violent phobic reaction was nothing more than the brain's determination to ensure the man's safety – in effect saying, 'I'll look after you, and I'm going to see that that never happens again, by making sure you avoid anything like it for the rest of your life.' Fear is a protective mechanism, designed with the function of delivering fragile humans from jeopardy, and it would be counterproductive to try to tough it out and deny all fear. The key questions are about whether your fear is useful or not: 'Is my fear protecting me or incapacitating me?', and 'Is it protecting me now, or is it just a habit?' And those questions do not only apply to individuals. Fear depends on memory and organisations have memories, too, which is why many corporations, institutions and even central banks often appear to be making the elderly generals' traditional mistake of fighting the last war, instead of the next one.

If you know what your fears are, you can know your weaknesses and potentially know what to strengthen to improve your life and your business performance. Assuming you took the time to draw up the 'five worst fears' list we suggested, you have in front of you a programme for action that could produce spectacular results. Each of the five items on this shopping list holds out the tantalising promise of a disproportionate, highly geared return, if you could remedy or alleviate its effects. If you could shake off the shackles of these five fears, you would be far better prepared to handle the shock of the new and the unexpected, and even to deal with crisis situations.

The claustrophobic manager calls too many outdoor site meetings, while her agoraphobic opposite number skulks in his office, sending out volleys of e-mails and expressing an unusual enthusiasm for the virtues of video-conferencing. The boss who can't get on a plane to fly anywhere is forced to spend far too much energy trying to manipulate the external situation to ensure that every meeting happens to take place in a location that can be reached by road or rail. The genuine technophobe may even be found carrying a laptop around, to avert suspicion, without ever using it. These are the extremes, the caricatures, even. But their problems are really not much different from most other people's. The problem, for all of them, is that living with their fears obliges them to go to elaborate lengths to try to control the outside world. That is a demanding, exhausting strategy, requiring constant attention and adjustment and leaving you even more vulnerable than other people to the impact of unexpected change. The better alternative is to identify your own hit-list of anxieties, separate the current and valid fears, based on today's realities, from those you have been nursing since your formative years, and take some positive action to clean up the unhelpful leftovers from the past that are spoiling the present and prejudicing your future.

➡ CHANGE HAS KEPT YOU ALIVE

This may mean seeking out appropriate coaching, counselling or therapy. It may mean examining these fear factors for yourself, recognising that they are obsolete, ungrounded in present reality and no possible help to you – and just deciding to shut them out of your life. It may mean replacing limiting beliefs about yourself with new ways of looking at the world that give you more confidence in your ability to deal with change. Just seeing a familiar scenario in a new light can sometimes transform your relationship with it. For example, if you think of yourself as being apprehensive about change, think about this. You are changing all the time. You are the living embodiment of change. The liver you have now is a new one, reconstructed without your noticing it over the past few months. Your skin – freckles and scars and wrinkles and all – is virtually brand new, in as much as it consists of a close copy of last year's skin, renewed, cell by cell, on a continuous, rolling basis. And there is nothing left now, except a memory trace in the unrecycled neurons of your brain, of the child who was frightened by a dog, rebuked by a parent or surprised by the noise of a firework and has since been replaced by the adult you. Change is vital for life and for self-renewal. Change has kept you alive. Change has stimulated you to achieve everything you have done that's worthwhile. Change is simply not the problem.

Perhaps the crux of the matter is that you're convinced you don't like surprises. Have you thought what life would be like without them? Would you really like to have everything so much under control, for example, that you received an itemised list of proposed presents every birthday and Christmas, for your consideration and possible veto? Would you honestly be happier at work if you never had an unexpected phone call or a chance meeting that led to someone taking an irritating task off your hands? Isn't part of the fun and pleasure of reading a book, watching a film or going to a party precisely that element of excitement and unpredictability about what will happen next and how things will turn out? To see surprises and unexpected events as inherently negative and threatening is to discount half the pleasures in life. Trying to organise your world to avoid them is a mug's game. Coming to terms with change and uncertainty is not about trying to make the world more predictable, but about making yourself bigger, more powerful and more flexible, so that you will not be left helpless in the face of unexpected happenings.

One step towards this is to start doing new things that place you in the driving seat and make you more aware of your own capacity to take initiatives. We have often found that people's self-assurance and resourcefulness are undermined by their feeling physically out of condition. Deskbound office workers who still think of themselves as young and energetic as they move into their forties may be heading for a shock when they suddenly start to fill out and put on weight. Many don't realise that a slowing of their metabolic rate is one of life's more predictable changes – and one that will be all too obvious if nothing is done to counter it, affecting self-image and confidence just as much as physical shape. Encouraging them to begin a programme of moderate exercise and resistance training, based on a cardiovascular workout routine and aimed at converting fat to muscle, has remarkable effects. Within two or three months, people report that they feel good and that their clothes are starting to fit differently. Because fat is being converted to muscle, there is a change of body shape, and with it a perceptible feelgood factor, as the understanding grows that the place where taking control really matters is in your own life, inside yourself, rather than on any external battlefield. If you can get that right, whatever approach you use, the unexpected becomes a source of interest and stimulation, to be welcomed as a sign of a future that you are fit and ready to meet on your own terms.

In a Nutshell   Expect the Unexpected

- **You can't control the future ... but you can be on your toes and ready for it:**
  - The Dictator's Fallacy is for control freaks, addicted to control.
  - But you can't out-control change.
  - What matters is how flexible, resourceful and creative you can be in the face of change.
  - What happens is important. What you make of it is decisive.

- **Think of three people you consider models of rigidity and inflexibility:**
  - Now think of three whose flexibility you've noticed and admired. Rate them out of ten.
  - Where would you rate yourself on the same scale?

- **Would other people call you flexible?**
  - Your flexibility is the guaranteee your people won't be wrong-footed by change.

– Being flexible doesn't mean you don't have a position.

- **Don't let fear stop you in your tracks:**
  - 'Who is this bad news good for?'
  - 'Is there some way the benefit to them can become a benefit to me?'
  - 'Does this mean that there is something I or we, as an organisation, should be doing to make the most of the changed situation?'

- **Those who work out how a merger can be made to work often get the job.**

- **Change creates opportunities, as well as disruption:**
  - The great danger is paralysis.
  - Take action – any action – to change your state.
  - Plan ahead: it'll take your thinking beyond the daunting present.
  - Activate yourself to activate the resources you need.

- **List your own five fears:**
  - Can you recognise how each has affected and limited you?

- **Is your past running your present?**
  - It won't make a good job of it.

- **Don't get stuck fighting the last war:**
  - Fear is a protective mechanism for self-preservation in the face of danger.
  - Is your fear protecting you or incapacitating you?
  - Is it protecting you now, or is it just a habit?
  - The five fears list is a programme for action with spectacular results.
  - Living with fear forces you to go to great lengths to try to control the world.

- **Change has kept you alive:**
  - Seeing the familar in a new light can transform your relationship with it.
  - You are new – the embodiment of change.
  - Don't try to make the world predictable; make yourself bigger, more powerful, more flexible.
  - Do new things that put you in the driving seat.
  - Get fit and feel better about everything.
  - Take control where it matters, in your own life.

Chapter 14
Where to Next?

'A single idea, if it is right, saves us the labour of an infinity of experiences.'

(Jacques Maritain, 1958)

➡ IF IT WORKS FOR YOU, USE IT NOW

In the chapters you have just read, we have made a point of selectively focusing on the areas of concern we have encountered most often when working with managers. Even so, it is a formidable shopping list. After all, when you are able to manage upwards, create a career path, motivate yourself and other people, get your own way, give valid feedback, use criticism constructively, manage all the resources available to you, handle those who are at a distance, lead, influence and delegate effectively, trigger greater creativity and bring out the best in yourself and others, you are going to be a very impressive manager. You will certainly not be waiting long for recognition and promotion.

But there is a lot to take in. There are a lot of variables to take care of all at once. Our suggestion is that you review the main topics and prioritise them for your own use by asking yourself: 'Given my circumstances, what is the difference that would make the most difference for me right now?' When you have identified where you can obtain the most leverage, you will know where to make a start. Why not cherry-pick? Why not take the easy gains first and make yourself feel good?

If you want to accelerate your rate of progress, it is worth considering joining a reputable NLP training course or even investing in one-to-one coaching sessions. If you work for a large company, however, you may well find that in-house NLP training is already taking place in other departments, divisions or offices. Our own detailed research shows that 18 of the top 30 corporations listed on the London Stock Exchange have taken advantage of NLP-based training or consultancy projects, while American giants such as AT&T, American Express, Heinz, IBM, 3M and Coca-Cola, and European multinationals such as Nestlé, Siemens, Volkswagen and Fiat have also tapped into NLP's restless search for excellence. A call to your organisation's central training or human resources unit may alert you to courses that are already planned. At the very least, most professional trainers and HR specialists are now aware of NLP's existence and potential and many would like the opportunity to introduce appropriate training into their repertoire of resources.

Organisations everywhere are becoming increasingly conscious of the need for New Managers who are not just younger versions of the old ones. The next generation of leaders is going to consist of people for whom the soft skills of communication, influencing, replicating excellence, creative thinking and self-management are as vital as the ability to use a spreadsheet, plan a project or chair a meeting.

The world will not go mad and people will not suddenly be appointed to positions of responsibility without the necessary technical knowledge to do the job properly. But the recruiters and those who plan management succession strategies will be looking beyond job-specific expertise in the search for proven competence in these crucial generic skills. Since, like any worthwhile capability, they take time and practice to develop and refine, those who see themselves as the New Managers for the new millennium need to be paying close attention to them now. Juggling all the variables, integrating what you do with what you observe and starting to think in ways that are sometimes quite counter-intuitive for people brought up in our business culture can all be challenging while the operational technology is still new to you. With practice and familiarity, you will become more comfortable with what you are doing, more subtle in your actions and reactions and less aware of each step. Over time, you will steadily move towards the ideal state of unconscious competence – effortlessly succeeding where you were once tense and tentative.

➡ THE TIP OF THE ICEBERG

There is an extraordinary range of useful techniques and insights that NLP can offer managers and those we have touched on in this book represent no more than the tiny tip of a very large iceberg. Beyond NLP Practitioner training, there is the Master Practitioner curriculum, covering an equally rich and stimulating set of skills and concepts, followed by many other specialised courses, and there is a wealth of material available for those who are inspired to make a serious study of the business applications of NLP. But your latent ability to see situations in a new and more helpful light can often be activated merely by knowing the right questions to ask yourself, so we have concentrated here on offering you some very simple ways to improve your performance by adjusting your thinking and your frame of reference.

➡ A FINAL THOUGHT

One question that is often put to us is where the dissemination of NLP is going to lead. 'What will happen when everyone in business is using the same techniques?', people ask. The question seems to be prompted by the notion that everyone will be using NLP to try to outwit everyone else. Of course, if that's what they are doing, they will have missed the point completely. If life is still a power struggle for you, then you probably have yet to enjoy the easier life that comes with developing the art of influencing. And it is influencing, above all, that NLP has to offer the world of business. So if everyone is going to be using NLP, we can probably make a number of predictions about the results.

One certainty is that there will be a great deal more rapport in the world of business and that a great deal of unnecessary abrasion and conflict will disappear from negotiations, disciplinary encounters and industrial relations issues. Another is that, as more people become clearer about what they really want, there will be many more opportunities to identify alignments of interest, enabling people and organisations to work together productively and collaborate to reach common goals. A third is that the rise of the New Manager, equipped with NLP skills and insights and the desire to lead, rather than control, will make the workplace a less threatening, more stimulating and inspiring environment for everyone involved. Customer service standards will automatically improve. More of people's abundant creativity will be released and channelled into new products and ingenious solutions to business problems.

There is simply no reason to suppose that anyone or any business will suffer. NLP is not a new technology like the Gatling gun or the napalm bomb, that can only benefit one group by harming another. It is benign and democratic, available to anyone who chooses to investigate the possibilities it offers. It is capable of boosting people's performance even in small doses, without demanding unrealistic levels of study and commitment, and routinely helps managers and others achieve outcomes they did not believe possible. As a result, a knowledge of NLP is a key resource for the New Manager, in the pursuit of excellence, job satisfaction and a secure and prosperous future.

'Go and wake up your luck.' (Persian proverb)

Appendix
Training, Tapes and Software

'Of the significant and pleasurable experiences of life, only the simplest are open indiscriminately to all. The rest cannot be had except by those who have undergone a suitable training.'

(Aldous Huxley, 1937)

➡ LEARNING THE SKILLS OF THE NEW MANAGER

If you are interested in learning more about how to apply NLP to get results in business, you will probably need to take an NLP training course. Because NLP is skill-based, you can learn a lot in a hands-on training programme that gives you the opportunity to practise the how-tos. However, many organisations have found it profitable to start offering some version of what they think NLP is. Beware! Ideally, check that the trainer has NLP credentials and that the organisation is recognised as an NLP training provider.

International Teaching Seminars is the UK market leader in quality NLP training. It focuses on the practical applications of NLP and offers a number of different programmes and formats, including:

NLP Practitioner Training – a comprehensive programme leading to internationally recognised practitioner certification. No previous training required.

First Principles – a three-day introduction based on the best-selling book *Principles of NLP* by Joseph O'Connor and Ian McDermott.

Professional Development Programme – divided into two short three-day programmes.

- Leadership: how to clarify where to go next in your life.
- Advanced Presentation Skills: how to use NLP to revolutionise the way you come across.

In-house Programmes – tailored to an organisation's particular requirements or to special applications, such as NLP and Sales, NLP and Stress Management, NLP and Customer Service. NLP and the New Manager is now available as a two- or three-day programme.

NLP Software – Goal Wizard
Goal Wizard enables you to define and keep track of all your goals on your PC, storing them by category and clarifying them so that they are realistic, motivating and achievable. It is ideal for identifying well-formed outcomes. With a team, invite each member to use it individually and then compare the results. You will immediately know where the gaps are.

Audio tapes
An Introduction to NLP (Thorsons)
What is NLP? (ITS)
Professional Development Programme (ITS)

Further details on programmes and products from:
International Teaching Seminars
73 Brooke Road
London N16 7RD
Tel: 0181 442 4133 Fax: 0181 442 4155
Internet address: http://www.nlp-community.com
e-mail: its_nlp@globalnet.co.uk

➡ ABOUT THE AUTHORS

Ian McDermott is a leading trainer, consultant and author in the field of NLP, systems thinking and personal development. His books have been translated into 15 languages. In 1994, he was made an International NLP Diplomat in recognition of his contribution to the field.

As Director of Training for International Teaching Seminars, he has made the practical benefits of NLP available to thousands of people, through public and in-house programmes. As a consultant, he works with many FTSE 100 and Fortune 500 corporations, including Cable & Wireless, NatWest, Prudential, TSB, BP, Shell, British Telecom and Coca-Cola. Ian is also a UKCP-registered psychotherapist and offers an executive coaching service that uses NLP to deliver rapid change easily.

Other books by Ian McDermott:

Principles of NLP, Thorsons, (1996)

Practical NLP for Managers, Gower, (1996)

NLP and Health, Thorsons, (1996)

The Art of Systems Thinking, Thorsons, (1997)

(all with Joseph O'Connor).

Develop Your Leadership Qualities, Time-Life, (1995)

Take Control of Your Life, Time-Life, (1996)

(with Joseph O'Connor and others)

Ian Shircore is an author, management coach and marketing consultant. He has tracked the evolution of the New Manager through extensive experience and close observation in the course of many big-company consultancy projects. He writes speeches for BT's directors and edits staff and customer newspapers. His clients include institutions such as the Treasury, London Business School and the Law Society, and businesses ranging from Sony, Diageo and ICL, to the International Herald Tribune. As a trainer, he specialises in teaching comunication and management skills, leading small-group courses for clients including BT, Ashridge Management College, the TECs (Training & Enterprise Councils) and the Human Capital training group.

Ian Shircore can be contacted at shircorebk@aol.com or on the web at http://members.aol.com/shircore

Other books by Ian Shircore:

Treasure Hunting, Macdonald, (1981)

Right for Your Reader, BT, (1994)

SmartOffice: 11 Steps to the User-Friendly Office (with Judith Verity), Bloomsbury, (1996)

Mastering the Internet (with Richard Lander), Orion Business, (1998)

Index

action plans, managing upwards 20–3, 27
added value 21, 22, 104–5
adenosine triphosphate (ATP) 82
advice 22
alcohol consumption 83–4
American Express 164
anger 58–9
appraisals 65–6, 68–9, 76
associative thinking 126–8
AT&T 164
ATP *see* adenosine triphosphate
audio tapes 168
away from bias, motivation 40, 42

bad habits 41–2
Bechtel 139
behavioural matching 58–9, 63
belonging, sense of 101
benchmarking 137–47
  excellence 145–6, 147
  organisations 137–41, 146–7
  yourself 141–6, 147
best practice, sharing 1
big picture 110–17, 122–3
body language 25
BP 139
brain 81–2

British Airways 138
British Telecom 152
Brown & Root 139

call centres 83, 102–3
car industry 1, 3–4
career paths
  current jobs 33–4, 37–8
  goals 30–7, 38
  ideal 143–4, 147
  managing 17–38
  promotion 1, 5–6, 17–28, 35–6
change 148–62
  control 149–51, 159, 160
  coping strategies 158–60, 162
  current payoffs 33–4, 37–8
  fear 152–8, 161
  flexibility 150–2, 160–1
  physical 159–60
  promotion 35–6
  reinventing yourself 23–6
Christie, Linford 89–90
'chunking' 110–17, 122–3
civil service 85
co-operation 55–6, 61, 139–40
Coca-Cola 164
coercion 61
communication

'chunking' 110–17, 122
rapport 6, 7, 8, 12, 56–9, 63
remote management 100–1
synchronized 10–11
teams 2
competence 96–7, 106
confidence 15, 96–7, 106
congruence 11, 13
connectedness 100–3, 106
contacts 21–2
control
  managing upwards 19
  motivation 45–6, 48–9
  remote management 94–6, 106
  resource management 83, 84–7,
    89–90, 92
  unexpected 149–51, 159, 160
coping strategies, change 158–60, 162
costs, career change 33–4, 37–8
creatvity 125–36
  associative thinking 126–8
  curiousity 133–6
  dreams 125–6, 128–30, 135
  guided metaphors 130–2
  training 125–6
criticism 65–78
curiosity 121, 124, 133–6
customer services 83, 102–3

day-dreams 129–30
De Morgan, Augustus 65
de-engineering, organisations 2
definitions
  leadership 110
  Neuro Linguistic Programming 4–5
delegation 43–4, 117–19, 123–4
detail 110–17, 122, 123
Dictator's Fallacy 149–50
difference
  action plans 21–4, 27
  old/New Managers 7, 14
  prioritising 163

promotion 1, 5–6
  search for 1–2, 8
Dion, Celine 128
direction
  choosing 24–6, 28
  remote management 103–4
disempowerment 61, 64
downsizing programmes 152
dreams 125–6, 128–30, 135

Einstein 90, 119, 126
Eliot, George 79
Emerson, Ralph Waldo 94
empathy 19–20, 57–8, 63
empowerment 48–9
  see also disempowerment
energy levels
  matching 58–9
  remote management 103–4
  resource management 81–2, 89, 91
errors, learning 68, 76, 119–20, 124
excellence
  benchmarking 145–6, 147
  capturing 10–12, 15–16
  models 4
exercise, physical 43–4, 82–3, 91,
    159–60

failure 67–9, 76
faith 103–4
fear 152–8, 161
feedback 65–78
  do's and don'ts 69–71, 74–5, 76–7
  feedback on 66–7, 75–6
  'feedback sandwich' 66–7
  identity 66–7, 70, 71–3, 77
  learning from 68, 74–5, 76, 77–8
  making it work 65–6
  motivation 50, 52
  negative 66–7, 75
  positive 66–7, 87
  taking 73–4, 77

Fiat 164
fibrinogen 85
First Principles (training course) 167
fitness 43–4, 82–3, 91, 159–60
flexibility
  change 150–2, 160–1
  enhanced 12–13
  getting your own way 59–61, 64
force 61
Ford 139
Forster, E. M. 1
'future memory' 40–1, 51

game plans, managing upwards 20–3,
  27
Goal Wizard (NLP software) 168
goals 30–7, 38, 54–64
Gracian, Baltasar 136

habits 41–2
Handy, Charles 154
health 43–4, 82–3, 84–5, 91, 159–60
heart attacks 84–5
Heinz 164
Heraclitus 148
hostility 58–9
Huxley, Aldous 167

IBM 164
identity, feedback 66–7, 70, 71–3, 77
in-house programmes (training) 168
incongruence 11
individuality 120–1, 124
influence 7, 56–7, 165
information, 'chunking' 110–17
International Teaching Seminars
  167–8
Internet 100–1
investment, self 35–7

Jonson, Ben 17

knowledge
  organisations 98
  people
    flexibility 12–13
    leadership 120–1, 124
    marketing yourself 19–20
    motivation 46–8, 49
    power 7
    remote managing 98
KPMG 139

leadership
  definitions 110
  flexibility 151
  remote management 94–5, 98
  style 108–10, 120–2
learning
  benchmarking 145–6
  feedback 68, 74–5, 76, 77–8
  mistakes 119–20, 124
Leonardo da Vinci 126
'less is more' 3–4
London Business School 66

3M 164
McDermott, Ian
  biography 168–9
  creativity 132
  fear 156–7
  NLP further reading 12
  remote management 97
managing upwards 17–28
  action plans 20–3, 27
  choosing direction 24–6, 28
  mapping systems 18–19, 26
  marketing yourself 19–20, 26–7
  reinventing yourself 23–6, 27–8
manipulation, dangers 11, 61, 110
mapping, systems 18–19, 26
Maritain, Jacques 163
marketing yourself 19–20, 26–7
Marquis, Don 54

martial arts 60
mediating, mindsets 2
memory 40–1, 51, 113–14
mergers 153
metaphors, guided 130–2, 135
Miller, George A. 113
mindsets, mediating 2
miniaturists 110–17, 122, 123
mistakes, learning 68, 76, 119–20, 124
models, excellence 4
money 46–7, 48, 50
mornings 80
motivation 39–53
    away from bias 40, 42
    delegation 43–4
    leadership 120–1, 124
    management 89–90
    money 46–7, 48, 50
    myths 44–7, 52
    self-motivation 39–46, 50–2, 53
    towards bias 40–1
myths, motivational 44–7, 52

National Health Service (NHS) 138
National Institute of Mental Health 81
needs 49–51
negative feedback 66–7, 75
negative phrasing 30–1, 42
negotiating 60–1
Nestlé 164
NHS *see* National Health Service
Nietzsche, Friedrich 125
North Whitehead, Alfred 10

objectives, getting your own way
    54–64
O'Connor, Joseph 12
organisations
    benchmarking 137–41, 146–7
    de-engineering 2
    guided metaphors 130–2, 135
    knowledge 98

mapping structures 18–19, 26
originality 126, 135
outcomes
    feedback 72–3, 77
    frames 87–90, 93
    orientation 12
    'well-formed' 32
overviews, 'chunking' 110–13, 122
'ownership', problems 48–9

'pacing and leading' 57–8, 59, 63
pain 80
pain/pleasure model, motivation 41,
    42–3, 50–2, 53
past experiences, fear 155–7
payoffs
    benchmarking 135–47
    current jobs 33–4, 37–8
    habits 41–2
'people knowledge'
    flexibility 12–13
    leadership 120–1, 124
    marketing yourself 19–20
    motivation 46–8, 49
    power 7
    remote managing 98
'people skills' *see* 'soft skills'
personal identity, feedback 66–7, 70,
    71–3, 77
Peter, Laurence 29
phobias 157
phrasing, negative/positive 30–1, 42
physical exercise 43–4, 82–3, 91,
    159–60
pleasure/pain model, motivation 41,
    42–3, 50–2, 53
positive feedback 66–7, 87
positive phrasing 30–1
powerlessness 84–6
practitioner training 13, 167
praise 50, 52
presence, establishing 98–9

price, career change 33–4, 37–8
prioritisation 44, 45, 52
problems
  frames 87–9
  'ownership' 48–9
product positioning, self 19–20, 26–7, 99
Professional Development Programme 167–8
profile, raising 21–2
projects, breaking down 50, 52–3
promotion
  making a difference 1, 5–6
  managing upwards 17–28
  self investment 35–6
property 60

rapport
  anger 58–9
  building 6, 7, 8, 56–8, 63
  improved 12
recognition 104–5, 107
redundancy 152
reframing 13
reinvention, self 23–6, 27–8
relationships
  management role 6, 8
  managing upwards 21–2
  rapport 6, 7, 8, 12, 56–9, 63
relocation programmes 152
REM sleep 128
remote management 94–107
  competence 96–7, 106
  confidence 96–7, 106
  connectedness 100–3, 106
  control 94–6, 106
  direction 103–4
  making your mark 97–9, 106
  recognition 104–5, 107
  teams 101–3, 105, 106
representational systems see sensory
  systems

resource management 79–93
  control 83, 84–7, 89–90, 92
  energy 81–2, 89, 91
  exercise 82–3, 91
  outcomes 87–90, 93
  small victories 85–7, 92
  stress 83–5, 91–2
  talents 79–80, 91
  time 79–80, 91
responsibility 48–9
risks 119, 124
role models 72–3, 138–41, 145–6
Russell, Bertrand 29

Saatchi 139
Saint-Exupery, Antoine de 108
sales professionals 1, 3–4
self
  benchmarking 141–6, 147
  feedback 66–7, 70, 71–3, 77
  investment 35–7
  marketing 19–20, 26–7
  product positioning 19–20, 26–7, 99
  profile 21–2
  reinvention 23–6, 27–8
self-delegation 117–19, 123–4
self-management 105
self-motivation 39–46, 50–2, 53
sensory systems 3–4, 12
'sharing best practice' 1
Sheets, Carlton H. 60
Shircore, Ian 169
Siemens 164
sketch-maps 18–19
skills
  motivation 46
  professional 17
  reinventing yourself 23–4
  soft 2, 8, 14, 24–6
sleep 81, 82, 125–6, 128–9, 135
'soft skills'
  capturing excellence 4, 10–12,

15–16, 145–6, 147
choosing direction 24–6
communication 2, 10–11, 100–1,
    110–17, 122
creatvity 125–36
framework 14
influence 7, 56–7, 165
rapport 6, 7, 8, 12, 56–9, 63
self-management 105
trend 2, 8
software, NLP-based 168
Spock, Dr 128
Stephenson, Robert Louis 39
stress 82–5, 91–2
success
    cloning 1, 3–4, 72–3, 137
    getting your own way 62
    keys to 12–13, 16
    motivation 40–1, 51
    symbols 31–2, 37
summarising 25
SWOT analysis 20, 27
symbols, success 31–2, 37
systems, mapping 18–19, 26

takeovers 153
talents 79–80, 91, 142–4
tapes, NLP-based 168
teams 2, 101–3, 105, 106

thinking, associative 126–8
time
    getting your own way 59, 63–4
    resource management 79–80, 91
towards bias, motivation 40–1
training
    company investment 17
    NLP-based 13, 163–4, 165, 167–8
    self investment 36
trial and error learning 68, 76

unexpected events, handling 148–62
Unilever 139
Unique Selling Proposition (USP)
    36–7, 38

value, added 21, 22, 104–5
visions, clarifying 99
Volkswagen 164

Williams, Esther 143–4
Wilson, Harold 59
work appraisals 65–6, 68–9, 76
World Wide Web 100–1

Xerox 138

Zeneca 139